EERIE COLORADO

EERIE COLORADO

MOUNTAIN FOLKLORE, MONSTERS AND TALES OF THE SUPERNATURAL

JACK DALY

THE History PRESS

Published by The History Press
An imprint of Arcadia Publishing
Charleston, SC
www.historypress.com

First published 2025

Manufactured in the United States

ISBN 9781467158411

Library of Congress Control Number: 2025934491

CONTENTS

INTRODUCTION

COLORADO'S SUPERNATURAL FOLKLORE

For those who enter Fairy Land, there is no going back.
They must go on, and go through it.
—R. Macdonald Robertson

When I was growing up in the small mountain town of Evergreen, Colorado, the supernatural seemed like an exotic and amorphous element of culture that was unlikely to affect my everyday life.

That was until I moved into a haunted house. After living in a place that my family and close friends unanimously agreed had, at the very least, an eerie and uncanny presence to it, I began to understand that the supernatural can exert itself in the lives of everyday people. It was no longer a vague or ethereal idea but in a sense something very real that changed not only my behavior but the behavior of those around me as well. It was not uncommon for a friend to stay the night for the first time, only to awake the next morning to ask me what was going on at the house. The basement, we all knew, was to be avoided.

Little did I know that beyond my own insular existence, the supernatural surrounded me at all times. The neighboring town of Idaho Springs has legends of Tommyknockers, diminutive mine-dwelling dwarves. Denver is full of other famous haunted houses and cemeteries. A nearby road in Thornton is known as one of the most haunted stretches in the country and is also rumored to be a portal to Hell. Estes Park's Stanley Hotel is the impetus for Stephen King's book *The Shining*. Many of the surrounding lakes have legends of water monsters inhabiting their depths, and Bigfoot sightings have been reported mere miles from my house. Even my own town of Evergreen is home to a haunted hotel called The Brook Forest Inn, which is said to be haunted by the ghost of a jilted lover and thought to be home to secret tunnels and hidden treasure.

Folklore and the supernatural are both aspects of culture that are hidden in plain sight. They are interwoven within the fabric of our lives but are often overlooked. The project of this book is to uncover the ways that supernatural folklore has shaped Colorado's culture, both historically and contemporarily. The book is bound by a single elegant thesis: supernatural legends in Colorado are local expressions of a wider folklore complex that find unique ways to express themselves in this particular cultural context. To demonstrate this thesis, I explore a wide variety of legends, broadly broken down into two types: the corporeal and the incorporeal. The corporeal legends include ostensibly "flesh-and-blood" creatures such as Bigfoot, Tommyknockers and lake monsters. The incorporeal legends focus on the spectral: ghosts and hauntings.

The endeavor of "placing" the supernatural in a Colorado context draws on the theory of oicotypification, which was developed by the Swedish folklorist Carl Wilhelm von Sydow. The term *oicotype* was borrowed from botany, where it referred to a plant variety that had adapted through natural selection to a specific natural environment.[1] For

Exterior of the haunted Brook Forest Inn. *Photo by Jeffrey Beall, Wikimedia Commons.*

von Sydow, the transmission of folklore goes through a specific process, as through variation and migration, the tradition involved modifies itself for new contexts. Von Sydow says of his concept: "When then in the field of traditions a widely spread tradition, such as a tale or a legend forms special types…the term oicotype can also be used."[2] This project looks at Colorado's supernatural legends to determine what about them makes them specific to Colorado.

As Alan Dundes notes, "If an item of folklore can be shown to have changed to conform with local aesthetics, ideology, values, and the like, then the establishment of an oicotype can be a vital datum for the identification of possible specific features of character or personality."[3] This book is full of supernatural Colorado oicotypes. To demonstrate how this is the case, here are a few examples. At Riverdale Road, Thornton's legendary haunted road, there are legends of a phantom jogger who appears next to a car, only to disappear seconds later. The phantom jogger is a local version of the famous "Vanishing Hitchhiker" urban legend, but what about it makes it a Colorado oicotype? What better way to have a Vanishing Hitchhiker in Colorado than to make them a jogger, in a state that values fitness and the outdoors. Or take for example the Tommyknocker. These chthonic creatures migrated to the United States from the folklore of Cornwall, whose miners came to Colorado en masse during the gold rush. However, along the way, significant changes occurred. In Cornwall, they were considered to be the ghosts of Jewish miners, but in Colorado they were thought to be the ghosts of specific miners at specific Colorado mines. This reflected a culture that valued individualism centered on the mining industry. These types of transformations occur constantly throughout the book.

Often when I tell people about the type of research I do, they are quick to tell me the supernatural stories that they know. They will tell me about a gate to hell in the town they grew up in or regale me with the stories they heard growing up about a haunted cemetery. These bits of local folklore, they seem to believe, are found only in the place they know it from. They are often disappointed when I tell them that there are hundreds of gates to hell and even more haunted cemeteries. This is the process of oicotypification: the movement of a legend from one context to the next. The analytical work is in unraveling what makes a version unique. There is a reason that legends occur in the places they do; it is our quest in this book to find out why the specific legends covered here appear in Colorado.

Most importantly, this book is filling a need, a gap in the literature if you will. There have been other books written about the supernatural in Colorado. However, they have been written by nonprofessionals whose theories and methods fall woefully short. Without naming these specific books, I can say that in general they leave much to be desired. Often, the authors merely present a folklore text, assuming that it is interesting enough on the surface. This is how nineteenth-century folkloristics may have been done: purely accumulating texts. What they do not do, however, is interpret the information. Folklore studies in the twenty-first century focus on cultural context. How are we supposed to make meaning out of, say, legends of a lake monster in a remote area of Colorado? That is the endeavor I have set out on.

Further, these nonprofessional books about Colorado's folklore are entirely unaware of a wider range of scholarly literature that would greatly expand their analysis. In order to explain what I mean by that, I will have to introduce myself, if you will indulge me. At the time of this writing, I am a PhD candidate in American Studies at Pennsylvania State University, Harrisburg, a school that has a long history of association with folklore studies. After spending two years on-site in Pennsylvania, where I was the recipient of the University Graduate Fellowship, I moved back to Colorado to complete my doctorate, teach university courses and write this book. I have a master's degree in folklore from Utah State University and have written, published and presented research on the supernatural. Beyond that, I have degrees in English, history and anthropology. This brief overview of my curriculum vitae is to not only establish my ethos but also reiterate the fact that this book interacts with the supernatural in Colorado at a more advanced level than previous work. In turn, I hope what follows herein greatly expands an understanding of the operations of supernatural folklore in this great state.

Another key difference in my approach to the topic is that I am neither trying to prove the ontological reality of the phenomena I am studying nor attempting to debunk it. Often the non-scholarly literature on this topic approaches the supernatural from a believer-skeptic binary. This, I think, is the wrong way to study the supernatural. I operate from a third position, starting neither from a position of belief or disbelief. I do think, however, that the latter of these two is more important. I don't assume a priori that the supernatural is imaginary. Much of the information I have included in this book comes from people I know personally who have had fringe experiences with the supernatural. It is paramount to studying the supernatural to not assume, as a researcher, to have a correct or totalizing understanding of how the universe operates. In short, I am not interested in the ontological status of the supernatural but rather how it operates on the personal and cultural levels.

This book is not meant to be comprehensive in the encyclopedic sense. There will be legends you as the reader may know that are not covered. This is, in part, by design. My approach is thematic rather than indexical. My hope is that the way I have treated these topics may inform you how to consider legends omitted and that the same questions that guided me may guide you as well: What does this legend tell us about our everyday life? How is this piece of folklore distinctly Coloradan? How is it connected to larger cultural traditions? How did experience shape this individual's understanding of the supernatural? Much of the preceding scholarship has taken this indexical approach but failed entirely from an analytical perspective.

A word should be shared, then, on my methodological approach. I have done my best throughout this work to use an ethnographic method, which entails interviewing people and engaging in participant observation. Throughout my work on the book, I spoke with people about their Bigfoot sightings, UFO encounters, experiences with ghosts, legend trips to haunted locations and more. What sets folklore apart from a field like anthropology is that I was not studying the exotic other but people and groups that I already know well. As David Puglia notes, whereas an anthropologist studies the unfamiliar, the folklorist studies the familiar: "not monsters from afar," he says, "but monsters lurking in their own backyards."[4]

Doing this type of work correctly requires a great deal of reflexivity. Studying the supernatural means thinking reflexively about one's relationship to the subject. As I mentioned previously, my interest in the supernatural was due in part to living in a house I interpreted as being haunted. The chapter in this book about haunted houses includes not only interviews with my own family but also my own auto-ethnographic musings on my own experiences. Beyond that, though, I find the supernatural to be inherently interesting. I am a huge fan of supernatural folklore and popular culture. My nights are spent watching documentaries about monsters and ghost hunts. I would be remiss to not acknowledge this crucial point.

While my methodological approach in this book is both folkloristic and Americanist, my theoretical perspective has been greatly influenced by folklore scholarship. More so than any other scholar, the work of David Hufford has been instrumental in my approach to the supernatural. Hufford developed his "experience-based approach" to belief in his 1982 book *The Terror That Comes in the Night.* In *Terror*, Hufford looks at sleep paralysis experiences and the phenomena of the "Old Hag," in which an individual would (A) have an impression of wakefulness, (B) become immobile, (C) have a realistic perception of the environment and (D) experience fear.[5] In Hufford's experience-based approach, an individual's understanding of the supernatural comes through personal experience. This position is surprisingly controversial to orthodox scholarship (often from history or text-based models), but I believe a scholarly approach to the supernatural is incomplete without recognizing Hufford's contribution. When someone tells you they had a Bigfoot sighting in the remote wilderness that caused them to fear for their life, what are you supposed to do? A historian may try to intellectualize it, but Hufford's novel approach allows a researcher to acknowledge that the experience had a profound effect on that individual's life.

Hufford's influence on this work brings up another crucial element: the element of genre. In our post-Linnaean world, we are desperate to classify and taxonomize. Folklorists are no different. Broadly speaking, this book looks at the genre of legends. In our popular nomenclature, we tend to conflate and misuse a series of closely related terms such as *legend*, *myth*, *fairy tale*, *fable*, et cetera. For a folklorist, however, these terms have specific definitions and usages. In this book, a *legend* is defined as "a narrative that takes place in historic place and historic time, that is meant to be believed or is at least believable, and has a 'weird' or supernatural element to it." Legends, then, make truth claims about the world. They interrogate what is real, what is out there. Legends express deep truths and are often generated through personal experience. It is through the art of interpretation, a deeply personal and subjective art, that meaning is made out of experience.

We can get even more specific with the types of legends we are looking at, though. Like Hufford, who interviewed people about their Old Hag experiences, this book also looks at personal experience narratives. Throughout the book, we examine these types of narratives, many of which have already been mentioned already but bear repeating here. We discuss, from my own ethnographic work, as some examples, a UFO sighting in the San Luis Valley; a Bigfoot sighting in Bailey; and a spectral encounter at a summer camp, just to name a few. These types of personal experience narratives, however, also have their own classification: *memorates*. Like the oicotype, this term was introduced to the folklorist's lexicon by Carl Wilhelm von Sydow and refers to a personal narrative of an encounter with the supernatural. So, while all memorates are personal experience narratives, not all personal experience narratives are memorates.

This book, then, deals with one of the most slippery aspects of the human experience: culture. During a discussion in a graduate seminar about folk narrative, I asked the class if we thought culture could even exist beyond the realm of the individual. In other words, we tend to think of "culture" as a stable category that neatly orders our world. The borders of our states are, after all, imaginary. This idea haunted me, much like the haunted locations of this book. Is Colorado culture even a thing? I have come to the conclusion that it is. While culture is comprised of individuals, who on a personal level incorporate their own thoughts, modalities and idiosyncrasies, culture is composed of this plurality. Having lived in several different states, I can say that culture is something. The culture of Colorado is not the culture of Utah, Kansas or Pennsylvania. Culture is transient and mutable. It is effervescent and as dissoluble as gas. So are ghosts.

The chapters of this book all reflect the central thesis that the supernatural in Colorado is shaped by the sociohistorical environment of the state alongside personal experience. The first chapter is about UFO sightings in Colorado. In this chapter, I drew on an extensive online archive of sightings. There are more UFO sightings in Colorado than could possibly be detailed in this book alone. Here, I use the research of the French astronomer Jacques Vallée and his monumental book *Passport to Magonia* to interpret UFO sightings alongside an array of supernatural and paranormal phenomena. I also look historically at the governmental inquiry into UFOs, specifically Project Blue Book and the more contemporary Advanced Aerospace Threat Identification Program (AATIP), which is at the center of congressional hearings. The declassified reports from Project Blue Book were a gold mine of information in the National Archives, but I also relied on ethnographic interviewing as well as my own personal experiences in dealing with this subject.

The second chapter focuses on Bigfoot in Colorado. In researching for this chapter, I developed a personal archive of over 130 Bigfoot sightings in Colorado. This was done largely through archival research and ethnographic interviewing. A unique insight generated through this chapter is that interesting trends develop when analyzing Bigfoot sightings through the lenses of the natural and the supernatural. Not everyone who has a Bigfoot sighting interprets it as being supernatural. This is to be expected, as the supernatural itself is a liminal zone of study that disrupts neat categories.

As is the case with every chapter, a Huffordian, experience-based approach is used to study these sightings.

The third chapter looks at lake monster legends in Colorado. I was able to identify no fewer than eleven lakes in Colorado that have legends about strange creatures inhabiting their depths. I draw on the work of scholars such as Lisa Gabbert, who notes that many lakes with lake monster legends also have stories about other strange elements such as hauntings or hidden tunnels, and Mark Fisher's concept of the "eerie," described as the presence where there should be absence and absence where there should be presence. The lake is a perfect place for a legend: it often sits on the boundary of civilization and the howling wilderness. Some of Colorado's lake monster legends are, essentially, "fakelore," or fabricated stories for economic gain, such as the Twin Lakes Serpent, or to a lesser extent the Standley Lake Monster. There are some, though, that are generated through personal experience, as is the case with the remote Lake Katherine in the Zirkel Wilderness.

The fourth chapter looks at the Tommyknockers, which were imported to the United States from Cornwall through nineteenth-century immigration. The chapter looks at how the Tommyknocker, previously called knockers, appeared in the folklore of specific mines in Colorado and transformed to meet the cultural mores of the gold rush. Through looking at historical records, interviews, popular culture and commercialized products, this chapter charts the transformation of Tommyknockers in Colorado.

The fifth chapter incorporates the medieval bestiary tradition to create a list of monsters in Colorado that did not warrant their own case study chapters, as did Tommyknockers, Bigfoot or UFOs. Inherently, there are a wide variety of monsters and cryptids in this chapter. For example, I include the Slide-Rock Bolter, widely considered to be Colorado's state cryptid. A cryptid, for reference, is a creature from cryptozoology, the pseudoscientific study of hidden animals. Most of the previous literature on the Slide-Rock Bolter purely describes its lore as a mountain-dwelling whale that likes to devour tourists. However, I take the step further and analyze the legend as being about the logging industry, deforestation and ecotourism. There are many interesting monsters in this chapter, including the famous Vampire of Lafayette, whose grave I visited and subsequently went viral on TikTok from a video I made about it (follow me there @thefolklord).

The sixth chapter looks at haunted houses. For this chapter, I cover what I feel to be the most famous (or infamous) haunted houses in the state. Many of these come from the Denver area, where the mansions of wealthy

The Tommyknocker Brewery in Idaho Springs. *Photo by author.*

early Denverites often acquired a reputation as being haunted, such as the Croke-Patterson Mansion or the Molly Brown House. To interpret this, I use scholarship from literature studies, which holds that often haunted houses gain that reputation because they look like an archetypal haunted house, and from folklore studies, which approaches the topic more phenomenologically through personal experience. Here, you can read my own memorates as well as those of people close to me.

The seventh chapter looks at Riverdale Road, which is reputed to be one of the most haunted roads in the country. Again, I use folklore theory to interpret, in the first place, why a road might be thought of as being haunted. Once more, we have the competing aspects of culture and experience. Symbolically, roads represent a journey, one might say in the case of Riverdale Road, a journey to the supernatural. Riverdale Road is home to an incredible number of legends, which I interpret as being Colorado oicotypes. However, I also do ethnographic interviewing to uncover people's experiential stories there and consider them as a form of "legend trip," which are journeys to places associated with the supernatural. Of course, I had to go there myself, as was the case for every place I could get to in the state while researching for the book.

The eighth and final chapter looks at Stanley Hotel, Third Bridge and Cheesman Park. My intention for this chapter was originally to make a classification system for types of haunted places in Colorado and to share a brief analysis on the places that I found for each. This quickly became an obviously untenable task, one that requires a book of its own. I found haunted legends from dozens of hotels and cemeteries. Instead, I chose to focus on three famous (or infamous) haunted locations while also considering why a hotel, a bridge and a cemetery might be rumored as haunted.

While this book has a single author, a book is not written without a vast supporting cast. It takes a village, so they say, and some thanks are in order. More than anyone, I need to thank my wife, Carly. Without her, this book quite literally would not have been written. It was on a hike

Dead trees frame the infamous Stanley Hotel. *Photo by author.*

A creepy dark tree stands tall at the Haunted Cheesman Park. *Photo by author.*

in the woods of Pennsylvania that after I voiced my desire to write the book, Carly encouraged me to just do it, despite the daunting climb toward completing a book. I need to thank many fellow folklorists who have been instrumental in my path toward writing a book such as this. My professors at Utah State University—Lynne McNeill, Jeannie Thomas and Lisa Gabbert—laid the foundation for understanding what this field of study is and how to approach a topic like the supernatural carefully and with sensitivity. My folklore professors at Penn State Harrisburg—Jeffrey Tolbert, Anthony Buccitelli and Mariah Kupfner—did wonders to expand my rigor as a scholar. Though not a folklorist, the encouragement from my professor Charles Kupfer in pursuing monograph-length writing helped me get over the initial reluctance to write a book in the first place. I want to give a special thanks to David Puglia, who advised me to work with The History Press to publish the book. His work *Maryland Legends* inspired me to write a similar book about Colorado. I certainly need to thank my parents, who have been unflinchingly supportive in my decision to pursue graduate education, especially in a field like folklore nonetheless. Finally, I need to thank all my friends who have been willing to share their experiences, their memorates, with me. Without their stories, this book would not exist.

I have written this book with a wide readership in mind. Although it is looking specifically at Colorado's folklore, I think the lessons and insights contained herein are applicable to the supernatural more broadly. Though I approach the topic with what I feel to be a scholarly perspective, I have tried to make my writing interesting and accessible. The supernatural is, in my opinion, after all, inherently interesting. This book should be enjoyed by anybody who is interested in the weird, the strange and the fringe. I do hope, however, that this book can make a significant contribution to legend scholarship, by looking deeply and closely to how legends morph to a specific cultural context. My goal is for this book to satiate both these readerships, the academic and the popular, by contributing a nuanced understanding of the study of legends and the supernatural, while also exposing my wider audience to the fascinating perspectives and discussions taking place in my field.

Finally, I must momentarily take off my scholarly cap and speak from the heart. This book is a result of what happens when you embrace the magical, the mysterious, the ineffable. The world of legend is all around us. My life is an enchanted one—a life where William Blake's refrain "to see a world in a grain of sand and a heaven in a wild flower hold infinity in the palm of your hand and eternity in an hour" rings with deep philosophical truth. It is a world where Wordsworth's "a sense sublime, of something far more deeply interfused" isn't just Romantic musing, but a guiding principle. So with that, it is time to take a journey into the unknown and cross the threshold into a strange realm.

PART I

CORPOREAL LEGENDS

1

COWBOYS AND ALIENS

UFOS IN COLORADO

Since immemorable times people looked at the sky.... They saw warning messages through meandering fireballs, bleeding moons, and eclipsing sons.... Man saw the Wild Hunt, the Headless Horseman, dragons and evil spirits flying with sparking lights.... People do not see these things anymore. All they can see are flying saucers.
—*Linda Dégh*

On a summer night between my sophomore and junior years of high school, a friend and I were walking around my neighborhood in Evergreen, Colorado. We came to a large meadow and saw something neither of us could have anticipated in the sky. A giant, glowing blue orb was flying above the meadow, dotting from one place to the next and moving in ways the likes of which I had never seen before. For what seemed like several minutes, we observed the orb until it flew off at an extraordinary speed and disappeared into the night sky. I interpreted what I saw that night as, by definition, a UFO. It was unidentifiable, it was flying and it was an object. It wasn't until years later that I realized flying orbs such as this have long been associated with the "spook lights" of fairy lore and have been variously called jack o' lanterns, will o' the wisps, ball lightning, short hoggers and forerunners.[6]

The first person to make the connection between fairy lore and the UFO phenomenon was the French astronomer Jacques Vallée, whose 1969 book *Passport to Magonia* shows, in extraordinary detail, the similarity

A news notice that depicts the celestial phenomenon seen over the German city of Nuremberg on April 14, 1561. *Public domain.*

between premodern European supernatural folklore and modern UFO accounts. This included the notion that fairies would abduct people and travel to their otherworld of Magonia by way of flying ships; that eating food given by the fairies or extraterrestrials led to disastrous consequences; and that encounters with the fairies and the extraterrestrials included gaps in memory or missing time. He noted the correspondence between crop circles and fairy rings; the preponderance of cattle mutilation in UFO lore and the fairy tendency to steal animals; and the similarities in description of these alien entities and the elves and sylphs of the Middle Ages.

A similar approach of comparing UFOs to European supernatural folklore has been followed by contemporary folklorists. Peter Rojcewicz observes that the Irish believed that the "Gentle Folk," as the fairies were called, originated on other planets, and the Tuatha De Danann, a supernatural race of beings in Irish mythology, must have come from heaven because of their superior intelligence.[7] The beings of UFO lore are also often described as coming from other planets and having greater intelligence and technology than humans. Like Vallée, Rojcewicz enumerates many similarities between traditional fairy belief and modern

UFOs, including the fairies' propensity to travel in fairy boats or spectre ships; their ability to manipulate their appearance, their "shining" bodies; and their role as superior beings, which has both positive effects (such as the ability to heal or impart knowledge) and negative effects (including assaulting and torture during abduction). Everything Rojcewicz described can be associated with both fairies and UFOs.

Thomas Bullard also notes similarities between traditional folklore about supernatural kidnappings and UFO abduction reports. Descriptions of alien abductions, Bullard argues, parallel folk tradition. This includes the theme of supernatural reproduction; warnings and prophecies about the future; and initiation rites that occur during the abduction.[8]

This approach is consistent with how folklorists have, and I believe should, approach the UFO phenomenon. In 1977, Linda Dégh, folklorist and pioneering legend scholar, wrote an article titled "UFO's and How Folklorists Should Look at Them." The folklorist, Dégh says, is not concerned with determining the "objective truth" about the mechanical operations of UFOs or whether they belong to the natural or supernatural world.[9] Instead, the folklorist should look at the UFO phenomenon in relation to traditional folklore genres and categories and as a legend complex that is in progress. In doing so, the task of the folklorist is to track the movement and behavior of the legend in society.[10] This is, of course, very different than the approach that of a UFOlogist attempting to prove the extraterrestrial origin of such encounters or a scientist trying to show the earthly scientific explanation of such vehicles. Dégh and Rojcewicz both show the epistemological problems that inevitably are encountered when trying to explain the nature of these reports. Instead, as a folklorist, I look at reports in Colorado of UFOs and extraterrestrials through the legend genre. While the term *legend* may have somewhat of the connotation of "unreal" in the same way the term *myth* is used colloquially, this is not how I am using it. Instead, the legend is a narrative that takes place in historical time and space, that makes a believable claim, and often with a "weird" or supernatural element. Specifically, the evidence I use often comes in the form of memorates, which are first-person accounts of the supernatural.

This brings me back to my own memorate that I shared at the beginning of the chapter. This was an experience that I had myself, an experience that to this day I still don't have an explanation for. This belies a crucial point. In UFO sightings, there is often what the folklorist David Hufford calls a "core experience."[11] Many UFO memorates are generated not through some free-floating idea mysteriously transmuting itself through "culture" but rather through personal experiences. Prior to encountering that strange orb, I knew of no such tradition in folklore. My observation was rooted in experience. Hufford is responsible for the most groundbreaking work in the field of supernatural belief, who in his 1982 *The Terror That Comes in the Night* articulated his experience-centered hypothesis, which holds, "Some significant portion of traditional supernatural belief is associated with accurate observations interpreted rationally."[12] The experiential approach can be applied to the UFO phenomenon, and Hufford says that the "ambiguity, along with its insistent claims of an experiential basis, should make UFO belief a prime subject for students of folk belief."[13] This approach has also been applied by William Dewan, who says of both Hufford's theories and cognitive anthropology that "UFO accounts may be understood more fruitfully to be based on real, unusual experiences that instigate a complex interaction between the event, existing cultural traditions, and mental schemas."[14]

This brief introduction to the folklore theory of UFOs is crucial to understanding how they operate in Colorado. Like every chapter of this book, my aim is to show how the folklore of Colorado is tied into a much broader tradition. In researching for this chapter, I have accumulated a personal archive of over one hundred reports of UFO and extraterrestrial encounters in Colorado, though I am quite positive that there are many more that can be found. My purpose is to apply the theoretical foundations of the aforementioned folklorists to the phenomenon as it exists in Colorado. This means that I will be using an experiential approach as well as considering Colorado reports in conjunction with the fairy lore of old. What results is a fascinating journey through space and time, to the Otherworld of the fairies and the outer space of the aliens.

UFOs IN COLORADO

Sightings of anomalous phenomena in the sky have been seen for millennia. According to the Roman historian Livy, who lived between 59 BC and 17 AD, in the winter of 218 BC Romans sighted "a spectacle of ships gleamed in the sky."[15] In May 2023, an individual in Aurora, Colorado, looked to the skies and saw "lots of lights spaced evenly apart like balls."[16] Sightings of "fiery globes" in the sky were common in classical antiquity. Seneca reports a sighting in 168 BC of "a ball…[that] was the form of a fire that appeared,

PAGE 2 THE CHICAGO SUN, THURSDAY, JUNE 26, 1

In These United States

Supersonic Flying Saucers Sighted by Idaho Pilot

Chicago Sun article "Supersonic Flying Saucers Sighted by Idaho Pilot," June 26, 1947. *Public domain.*

as large as the moon," and in the decade prior "a fiery red disk" was seen in the sky, "emitting a light so bright that it dissipated the night."[17] On two occasions in 1948, Harold Wright saw a green, soundless fireball in the sky.[18] In September 1950, an individual saw five objects in the sky at an altitude of five hundred feet while driving between Kit Carson and Cheyenne Wells that they described as "fire-balls" or "flying saucers." The objects looked as if they were made of glowing molten metal. The flying saucers flew at a speed of two thousand miles per hour into the air and disappeared from sight.[19] And in September 1952, Technical Sergeant Billy Ross Hughes reported to the office of Special Investigations at Lowry Air Force Base that he had seen five or six objects "wheeling in the sky in a circle about five or six times as great as their diameter."[20]

The similarities between the previous reports from Ancient Rome and twentieth-century Colorado suggest that the UFO phenomena has not changed drastically over the past two millennia.[21] The details of the UFO encounters and the terminology used to describe them have changed, however. The age of "flying saucers" began in June 1947, after an encounter by a civilian pilot named Kenneth Arnold occurred in Washington State. Arnold was searching for the wreckage of a C-46 Marine plane near the Cascade Mountain, when he saw a bright flash in the skies. Nine crafts flew toward Arnold, which he observed were flat "like a pie pan," with small domes and no tails, and flying at a speed of 1,600 miles per hour in a strange way "like speed boats on rough water." Later that day, Arnold described his encounter to a group of reporters, saying the objects "flew like a saucer would if you skipped it across the water."[22]

Leased Wire
Associated Press

Roswell Daily Record

RECORD PHONES
Business Office 2288
News Department
2287

Vol. 47, Number 99 Established 1888 — Roswell, New Mexico, Tuesday, July 8, 1947 — 5¢ PER COPY

RAAF Captures Flying Saucer On Ranch in Roswell Region

House Passes Tax Slash by Large Margin

Defeat Amendment By Demos to Remove Many from Rolls

Washington, July 8 (AP) — The house passed today the Republican-backed bill to cut income taxes by $4,000,000,000 annually for 49,000,000 taxpayers, beginning Jan. 1.

It goes to the senate where approval also is forecast.

The vote was 302 to 11, or more than the two-thirds majority needed to override a presidential veto.

The action, which may encounter another presidential veto, came after Speaker Martin (R-Mass.), personally appeal to the house to pass the bill by such a decisive vote— as to persuade the president that the people should have this delayed justice."

The measure is identical with one vetoed by President Truman June 16 as "the wrong kind of tax reduction at the wrong time" — except that the effective date is changed from July 1, 1947 to Jan. 1, 1948.

Congress leaders expect to have the revised bill on Mr. Truman's desk before the week ends.

The house passed the bill after the Republicans beat back a proposed Democratic substitute that would have reduced taxes by $3,379,000,000 and removed 4,000,000 low-income persons from the tax rolls completely.

American League Wins All-Star Game

Chicago, July 8 (AP) — The American league, pecking away with an eight-hit attack and ringing the bell with its pinch-hitters, continued its all-star mastery over the National league by coming from behind for a 2-1 victory before a standing room crowd of 41,123 at Wrigley Field today.

Woodburn Compares Farm Progress in Past Twenty Years

Al Woodburn compared Chaves county agriculture with that of 20 years ago, in an address to the Kiwanis club today, citing that soil fertility improvement programs have materially increased production.

As an instance he cited that 20 years ago lands in the county were yielding on-third bale of cotton per acre, whereas last year the yield was one and one-fourth bales.

The county is comprised of 3,866,000 acres of land, he said, from which the annual income is $20,000,000 on today's figures. Ninety thousand acres are under irrigated cultivation. Beside the

Security Council Paves Way to Talks On Arms Reductions

Lake Success, July 8 (AP) — The United Nations security council today approved an American blueprint for the arms reduction discussions despite a Russian warning that the plan would bring about a collapse of arms regulation efforts.

The vote was 9 to 0, with Russian and Poland abstaining.

In view of Russia's firm stand against the U.S. plan it had been believed she might invoike the big power veto to block it.

Soviet Deputy Foreign Minister Andrei A. Gromyko gave his warning before the United Nations security council in a new effort to revive the Soviet working plan which already had been rejected by the commission for conventional armaments.

His challenge was taken up promptly by French delegate Alexandre Parodi and U.S. Representative Herschel V. Johnson, who announced their opposition to any substitute for the American plan.

Gronyko insisted that no program for arms regulation could succeed unless the plan was linked directly with an absolute prohibition of atomic weapons.

He declared that the U.S. plan approved by the commission did not link the problems of arms reduction and the banning of atomic weapons and, for this reason, it offered no basis for a solution.

Gromyko opened debate on the arms question as delegates awaited another major declaration from him later in the day in reply to United States and British demands for action to restore order in the critical Balkan situation.

Delegates agreed they were approaching perhaps the gravest moment in U.N. history.

Gromyko said the U.S. program was not a plan bu merely a document outlining a series of broad generalizations. The Soviet proposals on the other had, he said, offered specific points which should be dealt with, such as the regulation of war production, distribution of armed forces and military transport.

"It is obviously," Gromyko added, "that the commission cannot work out a plan without linking it to atomic control."

This is directly contrary to the main principle of the U.S. plan, which provides that all atomic problems would be handled by the atomic energy commission and not by the commission for conventional armaments.

Some delegates saw in his speech an indication that he was preparing to invoke the big power vote to block council approval of the U.S. plan. Thus the threat of a veto hung over both the U.S. arms plan and a U.S. plan for stabilizing the disturbed Balkan situation.

The big question was whether Gromyko would invoke the veto to block an American proposal to set up a U.N. watch along Greece's northern border. Some delegates expressed belief Gromyko might give a definite answer to this question.

British Delegate Sir Alexander Cadogan already has declared that if the security council could not solve the Balkan problem, the United Nations might as well "pack up" and

No Details of Flying Disk Are Revealed

Roswell Hardware Man and Wife Report Disk Seen

The intelligence office of the 509th Bombardment group at Roswell Army Air Field announced at noon today, that the field has come into possession of a flying saucer.

According to information released by the department, over authority of Maj. J.A. Marcel, intelligence officer, the disk was recovered on a ranch in the Roswell vicinity, after an unidentified rancher had notified Sheriff Geo. Wilcox, here, that he had found the instrument on his premises.

Major Marcel and a detail from his department went to the ranch and recovered the disk, it was stated.

After the intelligence office here had inspected the instrument it was flown to "higher headquarters."

The intelligence office stated that no details of the saucer's construction or its appearance had been revealed.

Mr. and Mrs. Dan Wilmot apparently were the only persons in Roswell who have seen what they thought was a flying disk.

They were sitting on their porch at 105 South Penn. last Wednesday night at about ten minutes before ten o'clock when a large glowing object zoomed out of the sky from the southeast, going in a northwesterly direction at a high rate of speed.

Wilmot called Mrs. Wilmot's attention to it and both ran down into the yard to watch. It was in sight less than a minute, perhaps 40 or 50 seconds, Wilmot estimated.

Wilmot said that it appeared to him to be about 1,500 feet high and going fast. He estimated between 400 and 500 miles per hour.

In appearance it looked oval in shape like two inverted saucers, faced mouth to mouth, or like two old type washbowls placed together in the same fashion. The entire body glowed as though light were showing through from inside, though not like it would be if a light were merely underneath.

From where he stood Wilmot said that the object looked to be about 5 feet in size, and making allowance for the distance it was from town he figured that it must have been 15 or 20 feet in diameter, though this was just a guess.

Wilmot said that he heard no sound but that Mrs. Wilmot said she heard a swishing sound for a very short time.

The object came into view from the southeast and disappeared over the treetops in the general vicinity of six-mile hill.

Wilmot, who is one of the most respected and reliable citizens in town, kept the story to himself hoping that someone else would come out and tell about having seen one, but finally today decided that he would go ahead and tell about seeing it. The announcement that the RAAF was in possession of one came only a few minutes after he had decided to release the details of what he had seen.

Ex-King Carol Weds Mme. Lupescu

Former King Carol of Romania and Mme. Elena Lupescu relax aboard the S. S. America bound for Cuba and Mexico in May, 1941. A member of Carol's household in Rio de Janeiro said the ex-king and his companion for 23 years in reign and exile were recently married at their hotel Capacabana Palace suite. (AP Wirephoto).

Miners and Operators Sign Highest Wage Pact in History

Washington, July 8 (AP) — An agreement averting a nationwide soft coal strike was signed today by John L. Lewis and a majority of the bituminous operators.

In announcing the signing, Lewis told a news conference that it is "reasonable to assume" the entire industry will accept the agreement within a few days.

Washington, July 8 (AP) — An agreement under which 150,000 of the nation's soft coal miners will work when "willing and able" at the highest wage in history was signed today.

Harry M. Moses, representing the steel companies, and Charles O'Neill, of the northern commercial operators, signed for their operations employing the 150,000.

Other operators from the Midwest and Far West, who employ west and Far West, who employ an additional 150,000 miners, were waiting their turn to put their signature to the pact, negotiated by Moses and O'Neill in days of dickering.

The ceremony was held in Lewis' offices at headquarters of his United Mine Workers.

Only the Southern group of operators, producers of about 25 percent of the nation's coal, is left outside the ranks of those ready to meet Lewis' terms. Even they appeared willing to fall in line but called a meeting to talk it over first.

An official of the UMW told reporters union district presidents immediately started notifying miners to report for work at pits owned by the operators who signed the agreement.

The men have been on a 10-day vacation, which ended last night Lewis had told them to await the formal signing of the contrac before going back to the pits.

Lewis offered the contract to the operators on a take-it-or-leave-i basis. Its terms were made public by the Northern negotiating committee, with a statement declarin the agreement will "make possibl the quick return to full scale operations in the steel industry" and th coal fields.

It also will boost the cost of coa and "many products dependen upon coal," the president said, bu the operators are convinced tha the full-scale production it permit "is the most effective way to maintain the economy of the nation."

The contract, effective until Jul 1, 1948, provides:

1. A 44 1/2 cent basic hourl wage increase — raising miner pay to $13.05 a day — far abov 1947's second-round "pattern" c wage increases in other industrie
2. An eight-hour day, includin portal-to-portal time, instead of nine-hour day; also, a half-hou instead of 15 minutes for lunch.
3. A 10-cents-a-ton levy, instea of 5 cents, to support the miner welfare fund. The fund will be go erned by a three-man board trustees made up of Ezra Va

Air Force General Says Army Not Doing Experiments

Portland, Ore., July 8 (AP)—The Oregonian said today that Maj. Gen. Nathan F. Twining, chief of

A *Roswell Daily Record* article, "RAAF Captures Flying Saucer On Ranch in Roswell Region," July 8, 1947. *Public domain.*

After Arnold's encounter, the age of flying saucers began, though the term was eventually replaced by UFO, which itself is slowly being replaced by UAP, or "unidentified aerial phenomena." The year 1947 was a watershed moment in UFOlogy. Less than a month later, the FBI field office in Dallas reported that an object resembling a "flying disk" had been recovered in Roswell, New Mexico, and explained as a weather balloon.[23] During the years following Roswell and into the late 1960s, the investigation of UFO reports was largely a government task, as the U.S. Air Force instituted "Project Blue Book" to systematically study UFO reports. Between the years 1947 and 1969, 12,618 sightings were reported to Project Blue Book, which was headquartered at Wright-Patterson Air Force Base.

While this might sound like conspiracy, this is history. The project has since been declassified, and the reports are available through the National Archives. Many of the reports come from Colorado, and some of them mirror the flying disk/weather balloon explanation from Roswell. For example, in June 1949 in Tioga, Colorado, a civilian saw five objects flying in two echelons at a speed between five hundred and six hundred miles per hour. The reporting officer interpreted the sighting as "the possibility exists that the objects reported were a cluster of cosmis or upper air research balloons."[24] And in 1949, an individual from Manitou Springs sighted something that was "a balloon shape and silver in color," that Project Blue Book concluded was "a balloon from the US weather bureau in Denver."[25]

The most important government-sanctioned report on UFOs came from right here in Colorado, at the University of Colorado in Boulder. Between 1966 and 1968, the U.S. Air Force funded the University of Colorado UFO Project, tapping Edward Condon, former CU professor of physics and astrophysics, to lead an investigation into the possible extraterrestrial origin of UFOs. The project was 14,855 pages long, featuring 59 UFO case studies, many of which were from Project Blue Book, and had chapters by 37 different scientists.[26] Ultimately, the Condon Report concluded that the UFO phenomena did not warrant further scientific study, and the government age of UFOs came to a periodic close, until being revived in the past decade.

In 2017, *The New York Times* released an article titled "Glowing Auras and 'Black Money': The Pentagon's Mysterious U.F.O. Program" that detailed the existence of a secret Pentagon program called the Advanced Aerospace Threat Identification Program (AATIP), which received $22 million in funding between 2007 and 2012. The program was created to investigate Unidentified Aerial Phenomena and funded by billionaire Robert Bigelow at the request of Senate majority leader Harry Reid.[27]

A video was released with the bombshell article, which showed a "Tic Tac-looking object" that Navy Commander David Fravor witnessed off the coast of Southern California on November 14, 2004. While stationed at the USS *Nimitz*, Fravor and Lieutenant Commander Alex Dietrich were doing a training exercise when their radar detected "multiple anomalous vehicles" descending at eighty thousand feet in less than a second. The "Tic Tac" object was mirroring his movements; had no markings, no wings or exhaust plumes; and was "well beyond the material science and capabilities that we had at the time." Fravor and other individuals involved with the sighting testified in July 2023 at a House Oversight Committee, and the governmental inquiry into the phenomena remains ongoing.[28]

The article in *The New York Times* was written in 2017, with the "Tic Tac" object becoming a famous term in modern UFO/UAP parlance and lore. But in 2010, people in Colorado were also describing what they saw in similar terms. On February 6, 2010, an individual had a sighting of what they described as a "tiktac" near Hermosa, Colorado: it "was a metallica shapped [*sic*] pill object just hanging in the air. It looked like a vertical silver tiktac. There appeared to be no combustion and it definitely was not a balloon."[29]

While this section may have seemed like a bit of a digression from the fairy lore described in the opening of this chapter, we need to ground ourselves in the present moment of UFO research. It is often overlooked, I think, that the government has taken interest in the phenomena, and rightfully so. The terms *UFO/UAP* do not make claims about their terrestrial or extraterrestrial origin. Initiatives such as Project Blue Book, the Condon Report and the House Oversight Committee treat this as a matter of national security. The sightings detailed in such projects, however, mirror descriptions from classical antiquity and, in a fascinating turn, manifest themselves in contemporary memorates from Colorado. So after this brief grounding in "reality," let us now turn our sights to the mysteries of Fairy Land.

FAIRIES AND UFOs IN COLORADO

When people hear the word *fairy* today, they may think of the Disney version that has become so ubiquitous in popular culture. The image of Tinkerbell, a diminutive, winged, harmless magical being, might come to mind. The fairies of traditional folklore, however, are quite different. They are often tall, incredibly intelligent, possess supernatural powers and come from the Otherworld. In fact, British fairies were not even depicted as having wings before the eighteenth century.[30]

So what are fairies then? A classical description of the Gentry, or the Good Folk as they are often called, comes from W.Y. Evans-Wentz, the American anthropologist who received the following description while doing fieldwork in Ireland:

> *The folk are the grandest I have ever seen. They are far superior to us and that is why they call themselves the Gentry. They are not a working class, but a military-aristocratic class, tall and noble-appearing. They are a distant race between our race and that of spirits....I knew a man three or four years ago whom they struck down with paralysis. Their sight is so penetrating that I think they could see through the earth. They have a silvery voice, quick and sweet.*
>
> *The Gentry live inside the mountains in beautiful castles....The Gentry take a great interest in the affairs of men and they always stand for justice and right. Sometimes they fight among themselves. They take young and intelligent people who are interesting. They take the whole body and soul, transmuting the body to a body like their own.*
>
> *Once they take you and you taste food in their palace you cannot come back. They never taste anything salt, but eat fresh meat and drink pure water. They marry and have children....They are able to appear in different forms.*[31]

There is much to be extracted from this description. Clearly, the Gentry are very different from Tinkerbell. The description, however, is not too dissimilar from what we might think of modern extraterrestrials. They are described as a "military-aristocratic class," and we have already seen the connection between military and modern UFO reports. The Gentry can evidently paralyze their victims, and later we connect this to the phenomena of sleep paralysis and the Old Hag as described by David Hufford. Like extraterrestrials, the Gentry are said to abduct their victims and take them to their Otherworld.

Evans-Wentz focuses on the bodies of the Gentry, and this is where we must begin. Fairies, Peter Rojcewicz explains, have a "subtle body," which means they have "light changeable bodies, neither fully flesh nor purely spirit, capable of altering their forms at will."[32] Because of the nature of their bodies, fairies are shapeshifters that can manipulate their form. Not only are UFOs said to exhibit such tendencies, but in Colorado, reports of their inhabitants share this shapeshifting ability as well. In 2010, a couple in Fort Collins saw a large black triangle flying backward at low altitude; it shifted into a rectangular box before moving into a cloud.[33] On June 25, 2012, a woman with the pseudonym Lucy was staying in a rented room in Glenwood Springs. At 3:00 a.m., the witching hour, Lucy awoke to see a dark figure in her window. The figure shape-shifted into a spider and crawled outside, where Lucy saw four figures, either short and stocky or tall and thin, standing beneath a blue light.[34]

The bodies of both fairies and UFO inhabitants have been described as being luminous or possessing a glowing light. For example, Jack-o'-lantern, a figure from Irish folklore, is described as carrying a shining lantern lit with a coal from hell, and Joan-in-the-Wad, the Cornish queen of pixies, wears flaming clothes.[35] In Ireland, the *Sidhe*, the race of fairies, are

Fairies as depicted in Sir Joseph Noel Patton's *The Quarrel of Oberon and Titania*. *Wikimedia Commons.*

A traditional Irish turnip Jack-o'-lantern from the early twentieth century. Photographed at the Museum of Country Life, Ireland. *By rannpáirtí anaitnid, Wikimedia Commons CC BY-SA 3.0.*

divided into two categories: the shining beings and the opalescent beings. Both of these classes are "shining," but the opalescent beings are lit by a light within themselves. In the hierarchies of the Tuatha de Danann, the shining beings are lower than the opalescent beings, who are more rarely seen.[36]

UFO inhabitants in Colorado are also described as having a "shining" nature. An individual named Michael (pseudonym) who lived on a farm west of Colorado Springs described seeing ETs on the ranch on numerous occasions. He called them "the old wise ones" and described "elongated skulls and blue translucent bodies." Like the fairies, Michael says that these entities are ancient beings who are watching over mankind and will warn us about impending disasters.[37] Prophecies and warnings such as this are one of the core themes of alien abduction stories.[38] Other people have reported even stranger encounters with entities they interpreted as being related to UFO phenomena. In 1993, a man saw a translucent growing creature in their yard that came into their house and began running through the walls.[39] This is very similar to the black shuck and the spectral hounds of the British Isles. Like this glowing creature, spectral hounds appear in legends in which they overstep their boundaries and enter churches before disappearing in a flash of light. In Welsh folklore, Cwn Annwn is a spectral hound and inhabitant of the Celtic Otherworld. It is interesting that *The New York Times* article chose the title "glowing auras" to describe the Tic Tac object, as fairies are said to travel in fairy boats or spectre ships.[40] One of the early reports of UFOs in Colorado during the Project Blue Book era detailed a sighting of a ship with a "dark luminous glow,"[41] and in November 2022, an individual saw a "transparent structure about the size of a small house floating rapidly through the sky" near Trinidad.[42]

Fairies and ETs are both said to be superior beings who, depending on the situation, can either bring about positive or negative effects to the people they encounter. People who encountered fairies were thought to at

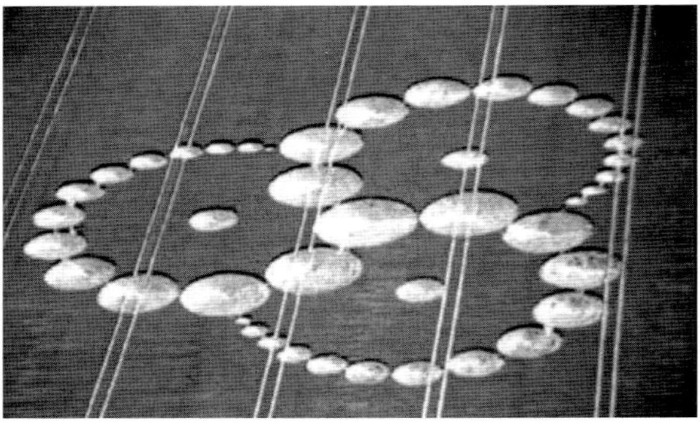

Left: A typical crop circle in the form of a triskelion. *Wikimedia Commons.*

Opposite: The Mowing Devil. *Wikimedia Commons.*

times receive magical powers, and fairy lore tells of a secret book of the fairies that could cure all diseases.[43] In 1980, an art teacher with cancer was driving from Denver to Longmont with his wife when he said a blue light shined on his car and levitated it into the sky. The couple lost track of time, as is often the case in fairy lore, but after going through hypnosis the man recalled being experimented on aboard the craft, and when they got home the melanomas on his legs had been reduced in size.[44] Encounters with fairies or ETs don't always have positive results, however. Often encounters with fairies result in personal doom in health, prosperity and personality, hence why the terms *Good People* and the *Gentle Folk* are used as to not upset the Gentry.[45] People are often driven to drugs or alcohol after seeing UFOs.

Of course, there is more to the fairy and UFO phenomena than the physical composition of the fairies' and ETs' bodies or the nature of their crafts. One of the most famous aspects of UFOlogy are "crop circles," the mysterious geometric patterns found left in fields, which often accompany UFO legends. Crop circles appear in many places, but they are most frequently associated with Great Britain, and attention to them has accelerated considerably since the 1980s, so much so that the House of Commons discussed them in July 1989.[46] Crop circles are especially analogous to the "fairy rings" of fairy lore, which are rings of mushrooms that fairies congregate at, where they dance and sing. If a child should come across such a ring during the dance of the Tylwyth Teg, as the Good People are called in Wales, they will lose their way and never make it out.[47]

Curiously, a pamphlet appeared in Hertfordshire, England, in 1678 with the title *The Mowing-Devil: Or, Strange News out of Hartford-shire.* The pamphlet details how a farmer believed a mower was asking for too much to mow his field and that the Devil would sooner cut his field than the

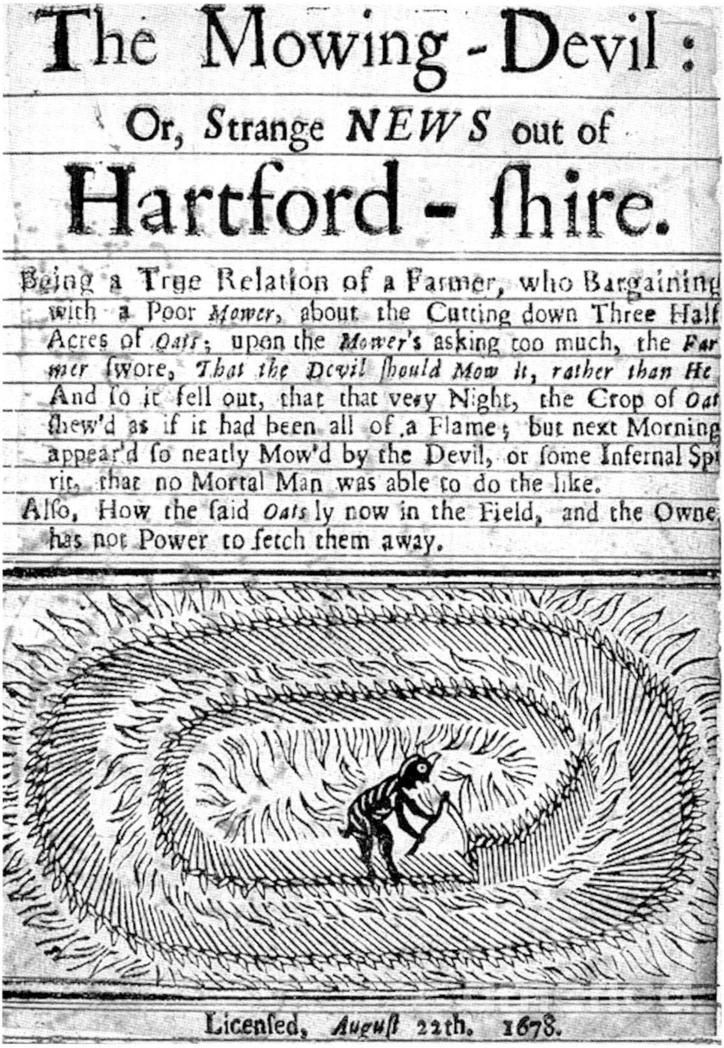

The Mowing-Devil:

Or, Strange *NEWS* out of

Hartford-ſhire.

Being a True Relation of a Farmer, who Bargaining with a Poor *Mower*, about the Cutting down Three Half Acres of *Oats*; upon the *Mower's* asking too much, the Farmer ſwore, *That the Devil ſhould Mow it, rather than He.* And ſo it fell out, that that very Night, the Crop of Oat ſhew'd as if it had been all of a Flame; but next Morning appear'd ſo neatly Mow'd by the Devil, or ſome Infernal Spirit, that no Mortal Man was able to do the like.

Alſo, How the ſaid *Oats* ly now in the Field, and the Owner has not Power to fetch them away.

Licenſed, *Auguſt* 22th. 1678.

mower. The depiction supplied in the 1678 pamphlet looks very similar to what we would call today a crop circle, but instead of aliens the Devil is to blame, who, like the luminous beings mentioned earlier, was once the brightest of all angels.[48]

The crop circle phenomena is not constrained to the oat fields of England, however. Like many aspects of UFO lore, it has found its way to Colorado as well. In 1978, John S. Derr, a seismologist, and R. Leo Sprinkle, a psychologist, detailed their strange experiences at a ranch in Colorado, which included the appearance of a crop circle seventy-five feet in diameter. Like the Hertfordshire circle, the circle would not allow crop growth directly after its appearance. Derr and Sprinkle reported an array of paranormal phenomena, including a strange hum (similar to rumors of the "Taos hum"), Bigfoot and UFO sightings, Mara attacks and cattle mutilations.[49] The reports from this ranch mirror legends from Utah's Skinwalker Ranch, which has generated so much attention as of late, and coincidentally was once owned by Robert Bigelow, the financier of AATIP. And in 1967, Mrs. Ted Wilden found two circles impressed into the ground west of Montrose.[50] One of the circles had polished stones at its center, and in France, fairies are thought to own luminous stones.[51]

One of the more infamous aspects of UFOlogy is the phenomena of animal mutilation. One of the most famous incidents of such mutilations occurred near Alamosa in 1967 when a horse named Lady went missing. The case is so famous that Vallée dedicated a section of *Passport to Magonia* to it, just two years after the event. A newspaper article ran with the title "Did Horse, 'Saucer' Tangle?" which detailed how the horse, which they mistakenly identified as "Snippy," (Snippy was Lady's mother) was found by Harry King completely skinned, with a precise cut around its neck, and no blood left in the body. They found circular exhaust marks in the area, though there were no tracks leading to the body. A piece of the horse's flesh was sticky and burned the owner's hand after she touched it. A forestry official checked the area with a Geiger counter and found the radiation count to be high, and a research investigator from the Colorado UFO project conducted an investigation. The cause of Snippy's death, the owner surmised, was from a flying saucer.[52]

Animal mutilations have their analogues in fairy lore. Evans-Wentz supplies the following story from his work on fairies:

> *A man was giving his cow water at a well, and, as he looked on the other side of a wall, he saw many strange people playing hurley. When they*

> *noticed him looking at them, one came up and struck the cow a hard blow, and turning on the man cut his face and body very badly.*[53]

These "strange people" are meant to be understood as the Gentry, who are also said to abduct horses and cows if not given milk and meat, and are often associated with wishing wells like the one mentioned.[54]

Another idiosyncrasy of the UFO phenomena are the so-called Men in Black, who in UFO rumors are quasi-government agents who discourage UFO experiencers from speaking publicly about their encounter. The "modern" Men in Black (MIB) legends began in 1952 when a Connecticut man named Albert K. Bender sent a letter to his friend, claiming to have discerned the mysteries of extraterrestrial visitations. After Bender sent the letter, so he claims, three men wearing black suits came to his home with his letter in hand, and afterward he stopped his UFO research.[55]

During the 1960s, the MIB were a staple of UFO lore, with John Keel detailing his own experiences with them during his investigations of the Mothman phenomena.[56] While the MIB may seem like a distinctly UFO-related rumor, Peter Rojcewicz argues that "with a better understanding of the UFO experience in general, the student of belief material is more likely to perceive the numerous continuities between UFO-related phenomena and various folk traditions."[57] With that in mind, Rojcewicz notes that historically, the Devil has been described as having black skin, citing Reginald Scott's 1584 description of the Devil as ugly with black skin, depictions in medieval manuscripts as a black human and Cotton Mather's Salem-era description of the Devil as a black man with the spirit of a poltergeist.[58] We could easily add the Mower of Hertfordshire to this list.

Legends of Men in Black were not limited to medieval manuscripts, Early Modern treatises, Puritan witch hunts or Cold War West Virginia. They also found expression in contemporary Colorado. In 1967, coincidentally the same year as Snippy's mutilation and of Keel's Mothman, an Alamosa woman saw a crescent-shaped object fly over the Great Sand Dunes. She painted a picture of the memory and later was visited by an MIB enquiring about the painting. The strange man told her he was from a different universe and could tell her the contents of any book.[59] This episode is eerily similar to Keel's stories of Indrid Cold, a man from his Mothman investigations who would descend from spaceships and deliver prophetic statements. In 2004, two friends in Fountain saw a metallic object fly overhead and were able to film it flying into some trees before landing in a nearby field. Subsequently, army helicopters flew toward the place where the craft had landed. Not shortly after, two identical men in black suits showed up at their house and interrogated them about the sighting before claiming it was a hoax and destroying their video evidence.[60]

While Men in Black rumors can be interpreted as being connected to classical depictions of the Devil, another phenomena of the UFO experience in Colorado is related to something both ancient and ongoing: the "Old Hag." One of the foundational texts in the field of belief is David Hufford's 1982 *The Terror That Comes in the Night*. In *The Terror*, Hufford analyzes the phenomenon of the "Old Hag," in which an individual experiences a sensation of paralysis during sleep (sleep paralysis), which is often accompanied by hallucinations of dark figures, a crushing sensation and an aura of fear. Hufford identified the Old Hag in places as diverse as Newfoundland, Pennsylvania, Sweden and seventeenth-century Salem, and it led him to develop his experience-centered approach to belief, which holds that personal understandings of the supernatural can be (but are not always) generated through personal experiences.[61]

The Nightmare, by Henry Fuseli. *From Tulip Hysteria on Wikimedia Commons.*

Hufford notes that the experiential theory can be applied to UFO encounters, though he also notes that interpretation plays a key role in how those experiences are perceived. He says that there is a specific connection between UFO abduction legends and the Old Hag, as many accounts of abduction include details of feeling paralyzed and seeing a strange presence in the room.[62] Some of the previous memorates shared may fall into this category, though they were not abduction accounts. Lucy saw the shape-shifting spider after awaking in the middle of the night. Though some of the memorates and legends I have found don't always include paralysis or abduction, the fact that they occurred at night after waking up indicates the possibility of an Old Hag experience. For example, in 2007 a woman named Erika (pseudonym) said her three-year-old daughter could not sleep because the previous night she woke up to see a little gray-skinned being with fangs and dark eyes in her room, which meets the description of a "gray" alien in UFO lore. What Hufford's experiential theory shows is that such encounters may be rooted in phenomenology; that is to say they "really happened" but there is a process of interpretation that the individual must go through to make sense of what they have seen. Having experienced the Old Hag dozens of times myself, I can attest to the strange and terrifying encounters that may occur in the process.

Hufford's observations on the UFO phenomena bring us to a central aspect of fairy lore and UFOs that I have hitherto avoided: abductions. The abduction phenomena has become such a staple in UFO lore that I hardly need to define it: an individual is captured by ETs, taken aboard their spacecraft and often examined in some way. The abductee communicates with the ETs, is given a tour of the craft and taken on an otherworldly journey; a "theophany," or encounter with a divine beings occurs; they are returned; and afterward there are effects that continue after the abduction.[63] Despite such ubiquity, the abduction legends are a relatively recent aspect of UFO lore. The most famous early abduction report occurred in September 1961, when Barney and Betty Hill witnessed a white light emanating from a disk-shaped craft that was following their car on their drive home in New Hampshire. When they arrived home, they noticed that the time was two hours later than they expected. After experiencing nightmares, the Hills underwent hypnotic therapy, which uncovered memories of being taken aboard the craft and undergoing medical examinations by ETs that communicated with them via telepathy.[64]

While such a story seems firmly rooted in UFO lore, it actually has much older precedents in fairy and supernatural lore. Like ETs, fairies are said to abduct people. They take both men and women, especially pregnant women and young mothers, but most importantly young children, who they will replace with one of their own children, which is called a changeling.[65] The underground and subterranean dwellings of the fairies, called the Otherworld or Fairyland, is said to be full of the people they have taken.[66] In the Otherworld, time operates differently, just like how UFO abductees often report missing time in their encounters. Those who are taken to Fairyland often cannot remember what they had seen or done there. Many Colorado abductees report such experiences. In 2001, a trucker suspected he had been abducted, as he reported seeing a bright light on U.S. 285 near Saguache and realized later he was missing four hours.[67] On a summer night in 1999, a man saw a reddish light in the sky and watched it for a few minutes. When he and his friends got back to their campsite, they could not account for three hours of time.[68]

Besides the events of an abduction scenario, there are other physical manifestations that occur in UFO legends that, although not always explicitly tied to fairy lore, connect them to broader traditions in folklore, mythology and religion. One example is the theme of reproduction.[69] This is present in classical mythology, where Zeus and other gods were known to come down from Olympus to mate with humans, as well as in the Bible, wherein the Nephilim are said to have mated with the children of men. Astonishingly, such legends exist in Colorado as well. In 1982, a forest ranger was called on a rescue mission during a winter storm in the mountains. When he got to his position, he saw a strange man and a blonde woman wearing a translucent gown. The woman drove him back to her cabin on a snowmobile, where she seduced him. The next morning, she was gone, but like Odysseus in Circe's captivity, two days had passed. Later, the woman appeared in his yard with a child and pointed to her stomach, indicating the child was his, but when he chased after her she disappeared.[70]

A final point I want to discuss in the similarities between UFOs and broader traditions are the implants left in abductee's bodies. Often, some sort of mark is left on an individual who has had a UFO encounter. For example, a 2007 article in *The Denver Post* details how a Yuma man saw a UFO in 1978 and twenty years later found a metal chip in his left wrist.[71] This mark is similar to the phenomena of stigmata, in which Christian mystics develop wounds on their body that mirror the piercings of Christ on the cross. While the UFO implant may seem like a profane example of that sacred wound, I would argue that the implant is actually a theophanous mark, a manifestation of an encounter with the numinous Beyond.

SAN LUIS VALLEY UFO

A final UFO sighting comes from an interview I conducted with my friend Andy, who saw an anomalous flying vehicle in the San Luis Valley, which is one of Colorado's most active UFO hotspots and home to the famous UFO Watchtower. Following Hufford and Dewan, this memorate shows that UFO sightings can be generated through personal experiences interpreted "rationally." Andy provided the following narrative:

> *I start seeing something come in from the north to the south, kind of going from the northwest to the southeast....My eyes are locked on in because it looks like a big helicopter coming towards us with a big, big amber light, and I'm waiting to see the flashers that a helicopter or a plane would have. I don't see any flashers; it's just a big amber light, and it's relatively low and it's cruising pretty fast, which is why I thought it was a helicopter and not a plane. I wait for it for a little bit to change trajectory, so if there was a flasher on a wing or on another side that it would maybe reveal itself as it turned. And after a while I didn't see a flasher, so with eyes locked on it I interrupt Aaron from his story and I say, "OK I hate to interrupt you, but what is that?" And I just point to it, and he turns around and he goes, "Oh that's a..." and just freezes. And I'm like, "See? That's a what?" and he couldn't come up with anything that it was....He was at a loss for words and literally went speechless....And I was like, "That's a UFO, that means that's a UFO, we don't know what we're seeing!"*

Photo from the UFO Watchtower. *Taken by Andy Olson, used with permission.*

Andy's memorate exemplifies what Diane Goldstein refers to as the "narrative witness stand," in which such narratives are "told as though one were on the witness stand, detailed and careful, incorporating numerous strategies that outline the nature of the observations, the testing of alternative explanations, and often includ[e] an indication of reluctance to interpret what occurred as 'supernatural.'"[72] Andy includes geographic details, such as the direction the object was traveling; is initially reluctant to interpret it as a UFO, doing so only when other explanations are ruled out; and makes no mention of the sighting being "supernatural" in character.

Such an approach should be applied to memorates in general, not just ones dealing with UFOs. There is a tendency to label anomalous encounters as outright lies, but personal narratives seem to prove otherwise. They are based off of personal experience and are often interpreted and reported in ways a person on trial might act: with attention to detail and reluctance to deem their experience as "supernatural."

CONCLUSION

Colorado's UFO encounters tie them not to just broader contemporary governmental inquiries such as Project Blue Book, the Condon Report and AATIP, but to larger traditions of supernatural folklore. This can be seen most startlingly through their similarities to traditional fairy lore. Coloradans report seeing shining entities that resemble the shining and opalescent Sidhe. Both the ships and the beings themselves shapeshift, like the fairies of Europe. Witnesses are at times abducted, taken on a trip to the Otherworld, lose track of time in the process and are left with physical marks on their bodies. Many of the extravagant stories of UFO experiencers in Colorado tie them to larger folklore traditions, but their memorates suggest they are rooted in personal experience. Work such as this demonstrates how even our seemingly "modern" folklore is often a transmutation of something much more ancient.

2

"WE'RE GOING TO DIE TONIGHT"

BIGFOOT IN COLORADO

I realized the folly of trying to measure the circle from some distant point, so I picked a microcosm on the edge of the circle—a place where many manifestations were occurring simultaneously and I hit the jackpot immediately.
—John Keel

In October 2024, several friends sent me a viral video on Instagram that purported to show a Bigfoot captured on camera in Colorado. The video, originally taken by user @bt92travels, was shared to the popular Instagram page @outtherecolorado. It was taken on a scenic train ride from Durango to Silverton in southeastern Colorado, near the San Juan National Forest. The footage shows what appears to be a tall, hairy creature walking along the side of a mountain, squatting down and blending in with the flora. A voice in the video can be heard saying "it's an elusive creature, [it] just squatted down." The post on @outtherecolorado's page was accompanied by the caption "Riders on the Durango and Silverton Narrow Gauge Railroad may have spotted Bigfoot on a mountainside in remote Colorado over the weekend. Thoughts?"[73] At the time of this writing, the post has 268,000 likes, 12,400 comments and 294,000 shares. The viral clip became so popular that TMZ wrote an article about it with the title "Bigfoot Sighting in Colorado Shows Clear Video of 'Sasquatch' Walking."

Whether this video shows an actual Bigfoot walking in the mountains of Colorado, or if it is what folklorists refer to as "pseudo-ostension,"

Patterson-Gimlin footage. *Public domain.*

or a hoax, is unclear. What the video does point to is the ambiguity inherent in the legend genre and, by extension, the Bigfoot phenomena. Although the video shows a clear image of a hairy creature walking across a mountain, it is far from definitive proof of Bigfoot's existence. The inconclusive nature of video evidence has been a central aspect of Bigfoot's mythos since 1967, when Roger Patterson and Bob Gimlin recorded footage of a reputed Bigfoot in the famous Patterson-Gimlin film. Despite the film *evidence* of these creatures, the ambiguity remains: it *might* be a man in a suit. The folklorist Linda Milligan highlights this point, arguing that in legends, there are often nonbelievers and believers, resulting in an inherent ambiguity.[74] In regards to Bigfoot, there is positive evidence that points to its existence, such as video and footprints, as well as negative evidence, such as the lack of a physical specimen, pointing to its nonexistence.

Milligan argues that folklorists should operate from a middle ground, resisting the urge to resolve these ambiguities, and in doing so learn about the Bigfoot legend.[75] It is from this middle ground that I choose to operate. Instead of investigating Bigfoot in Colorado from one of the two poles that Milligan identifies, which start with the assumption that Bigfoot either exists or does not. I approach this topic with the position that such a creature *could* exist and that people who report encounters with it are being truthful and rational.

Such a position was articulated by the folklorist David Hufford, whose pioneering work on folk belief in the supernatural resulted in what he termed the experiential source hypothesis of belief.[76] In his article "Humanoids and Anomalous Lights: Taxonomic and Epistemological Problems," Hufford argues for an application of this approach to large hair-covered bipeds, or what he terms ABSM, for Abominable Snowman, a term that encompasses these abominable snowmen, wild men, sasquatch and Bigfoot.[77] For this chapter, I will be using the term *Bigfoot*, as this is typically what my informants call the being, though it is used interchangeably at times with Sasquatch, despite the fact that these terms have different origins and usages.

Hufford argues that starting from a position of disbelief regarding "belief materials" such as legends and memorates is problematic because it assumes that the folklorist, or the documenter of belief, has the correct understanding of how the world operates. Hufford says that this position might result in the imposition of "a set of blinders which are derived from our assumptive set."[78] In other words, when a folklorist starts from the position that people who report Bigfoot sightings are wrong

The author at Wellington Lake, rumored to be a Bigfoot hotspot. *Photo by author.*

or misinterpreting experience, they (the folklorist or ethnographer) are also imposing their own worldview onto the situation, which is in itself a form of belief. Hufford cites that meteorites, the giant squid and the African gorilla all began as folklore, until they were verified as scientific fact. He argues that if we treat Bigfoot as not existing despite eyewitness testimony, we run the risk of the same error astronomers made in the eighteenth century when farmers reported meteorites on their land. Without visiting the site, astronomers assumed that the presence of meteorites could not be the case and instead posited that the farmers had failed to note the giant boulders before.[79]

Photograph of an alleged yeti footprint found by Michael Ward. Photograph was taken at Menlung glacier on the Everest expedition by Eric Shipton in 1951. *"The World's Most Mysterious Footprints,"* Popular Science, *December 1952. Public domain.*

Joshua Blu Buhs takes the opposite position of Hufford in his book *Bigfoot: The Life and Times of a Legend*. Buhs treats Bigfoot as a metaphor and a character who represents cultural ideas. The thesis of the book is that "maybe there is no Bigfoot walking the forests of the American Pacific Northwest, but the creature is still *real*—it is part of the American cultural landscape."[80] Such an approach, Buhs argues, allows for us to understand broad cultural processes during the twentieth century. Such an approach is fine in its own right, but as Yasmine Musharbash argues, the metaphorical approach breaks down when people report actually seeing or experiencing a monster.[81] In memorates about Bigfoot encounters, these are not metaphors, but using Milligan's middle-ground approach allows the researcher to dig further into what is being expressed in these narratives beyond the sighting itself.

A BRIEF HISTORY OF BIGFOOT

Stories about wild, hairy humanoids are quite ancient. The *Epic of Gilgamesh* tells of Enkidu, a wild man and companion of Gilgamesh, while Esau in the Bible is covered in animal hair and has an offensive odor, much like modern-day Bigfoot reports.[82] Medieval European tradition is full of Wild Men, who resemble contemporary Bigfoot both in physical descriptions and in behavior.[83] Hufford argues that modern interest in these creatures was accelerated in 1921, when Lieutenant Colonel Howard Bury returned from climbing Mount Everest and reported seeing a large creature walking in the snow at sixteen thousand feet. A reporter took interest in the story and uncovered Himalayan tradition about large hairy bipeds. The name *abominable snowman* was given to the creature, which was a mistranslation of the Nepalese Kang-Mi, referring to the high altitudes at which the being prefers to live.[84]

Wild man brandishing an uprooted tree trunk, design for a glass-painting; with foliage around his head and waist, holding tree trunk with both hands, mountains and trees behind, framed by columns and an ornamented arch, circa 1528. By Hans Holbein the Younger (1497/1498–1543). *Public domain.*

Bigfoot's breakthrough came in 1958 in Bluff Creek, California. A bulldozer operator named Jerry Crew found giant footprints at his road construction work site, which were then cast in plaster. These footprints became a media sensation, with headlines in California dubbing the prints' creator "Bigfoot." This original case has a layer of question around it, however, as it was later revealed that Ray Wallace, a worker at Crew's site, had created the footprints.[85]

Arguably the most famous piece of Bigfoot footage came nearly a decade after the Bluff Creek incident, ironically in the same area. On October 20, 1967, Rober Patterson and Bob Gimlin recorded footage of a large, hairy biped walking along a creek bed in Bluff Creek. This infamous piece of film has become known as "The Patterson-Gimlin Film." Whether or not the creature in the film is an actual Bigfoot or not is fiercely debated, but it returns us to the original point: that there is an inherent ambiguity in the Bigfoot legend.

Hufford argues that the long history of stories about wild, hairy humanoids leaves us with two options. He says, "Either there is an ancient tradition of such creatures which has been far more persistent, widespread and conservative than anyone has seriously considered; or the accounts are based on an objectively real referent, sometimes embedded in a tradition and sometimes not, perhaps depending on the frequency of sightings in a given place and time."[86] In other words, the stability of Bigfoot/ABSM descriptions across thousands of years either means that this is a traditional story that has maintained stable features that haven't changed greatly, or they are based off a creature who is being sighted in the wild but is not yet identified by science. Ultimately, Hufford argues that we must approach belief "with respect for our informants and a taxonomy which does not mistake our own epistemological systems for objective reality, nor those of our informants for a prelogical dream world where subject and object cannot be distinguished.[87]

BIGFOOT IN COLORADO

This introduction to Bigfoot theory and history allows me to clarify my approach to the topic as well as the general argument of the book. I operate from the "tradition of belief," which focuses on human testimony and personal experience narratives such as memorates.[88] This does not mean that I necessarily believe these legends to be true, but what it does mean is that I don't start from a position of disbelief. The main premise of this book is that the folklore of Colorado is a regional expression of larger traditions of folklore and storytelling. In the case of Bigfoot, Colorado is a hotspot for stories of the creature.

The history of Bigfoot in Colorado aligns with Hufford's observations that traditions of wild, hairy humanoid beings may be the result of personal experiences rather than free-floating cultural ideas. As previously noted, the term *Bigfoot* wasn't used until the 1950s, and the Bigfoot phenomena really solidified its popularity in American culture during that period. In Colorado, however, people reported seeing creatures that resemble Bigfoot as early as the 1880s, long before there was an agreed-on terminology to describe such beings.

In 1880, two newspaper articles appeared in *The Rocky Mountain News* and *The Gunnison Democrat* that detailed an experience that miners had at Grizzly Peak near Leadville with a strange creature that was described as half man and half beast (an orangutan specifically) that was covered in hair, had eyes like glowing coals and emitted a moaning noise that terrified the miners. The first story from the November 3, 1880 edition of *The Rocky Mountain News* had the title "A Monster Seen in the Mountains Near Grizzly Peak. Half a Man and Half a Beast. A Rival to the Centaur of Old." The article described their terrifying experience:

> *For some time past the miners in the vicinity of Grizzly peak, about forty miles south-east of this city, have reported the presence of a strange animal different from anything known in the mountains.*
>
> *On a number of different occasions a creature, resembling a man, save for the extraordinary length of arms, and the long shaggy hair that covered the body, has been seen at a distance among the rocks.*
>
> *At first its existence was supposed to be a myth, and the miner who brought in the story was hooted at and generally disbelieved. Finally, however, there were so many witnesses that it became an undenied fact that a wild animal, totally different from anything known to science or natural history, existed somewhere amidst the rocky lairs of the adjoining mountains....*
>
> *He saw, crouched behind a huge stone, a thing that had the semblance of a man, and yet was more than half a beast. The body was heavily built and proportioned something as an orangoutang* [sic], *particularly in the long and extraordinarily muscular arms. The face, however, would have struck terror into the bravest of men. An almost human countenance, covered with coarse, brown hair, similar to that with which the whole body was clothed, was made ferocious by a pair of eyes that glowed like living coals.*[89]

Many aspects of this report are interesting in that the reporter and the miners themselves are struggling to put into words what it is they saw, and yet the sighting is consistent with modern Bigfoot descriptions. The creature is described as being ape-like, with large muscular arms and an almost human countenance but also terrifying, strange and monstrous. Even the moaning noise is reminiscent of contemporary Bigfoot lore, such as the infamous Sierra Sounds, the reputed howls of a Bigfoot recorded in California in the 1970s.

Two weeks later, on November 17, 1880, a story ran in *The Gunnison Democrat* with the title "Half Man and Half Beast."[90] These articles conform with Hufford's arguments regarding Bigfoot-like creatures, in that they resemble both older traditions of hairy humanoid creatures and contemporary accounts. The articles predate the coinage of the term *Bigfoot* by almost eighty years, yet the descriptions are nearly identical. Here we see a description of an ape-like creature that is large and menacing and unlike anything hitherto identified by science.

Outside of historic newspaper articles, a great source for Bigfoot narratives is the Bigfoot Field Researchers Organization (BFRO), which has an online archive that is invaluable for Bigfoot research. The archive has documentation of Bigfoot sightings for every state in the country, with county-by-county breakdowns. Their website categorizes sightings as either Class A, sightings in circumstances where misinterpretation or misidentification of other animals can be ruled out with greater confidence; Class B, incidents where a possible sasquatch was observed at a great distance or in poor lighting conditions and incidents in any other circumstance that did not afford a clear view of the subject; and Class C, secondhand reports and any thirdhand reports, or stories with an untraceable sources.[91] In Colorado, the BFRO has a total of 130 reports. Park County has the most sightings reported with 13; and El Paso County has the most Class A reports with 6. The oldest report comes from 1926 in Jackson County, and the most recent is from Hinsdale County in 2021.

The oldest report, from Jackson County, was submitted by the daughter of a man who saw two large hairy creatures walking bipedally near the town of Walden in 1926.[92] Many of the reports I have read over through the BFRO database start with the creatures looking something like a bear. Inevitably, something occurs that changes the observer's mind to interpret their experience as a Bigfoot. In this case, it was that the creatures began to walk bipedally while stalking an elk.

In researching for this book, I read every Class A report in the BFRO Colorado database. What struck me is that even the most credible encounters did not come straight out and say something along the lines of "this was Bigfoot—there's absolutely no doubt in that." The reports expressed some sort of ambivalence in their narrations. Often, people said they first interpreted what they were seeing as a bear but were convinced that it was a Bigfoot based on some sort of anomalous feature of the sighting, such as seeing the creature walk bipedally. Bears, of course, can walk on two legs, so seeing a hairy creature do this does not mean it is not a bear.

The fact that people expressed ambivalence in their reports does not mean what they encountered was not a Bigfoot; this could actually strengthen the veracity of their experiences. By displaying a certain amount of skepticism, these individuals are showing that they were thinking critically about what they were seeing. The use of rhetorical strategies such as providing other possible explanations, testing, corroborating testimony and a hesitancy to speak about an encounter are all methods used by narrators to increase the plausibility of their story.[93] Such is the case of Colorado Bigfoot narratives.

Some of the most convincing sighting reports come from people trained in close observation and wilderness survival. For example, a former Marine reported seeing a tall creature in 1986 near Fort Carson that he described in the following way: "[It was] covered in light brown fur, had large fox-like ears, and large, black, globe-shaped eyes. The nostrils were slitted and large, without much nasal definition. The body was muscular, with a thin waist and easily discernible definition, and the arms were long, hanging below the level of the hips." Similarly, a former deputy sheriff described a sighting from Conejos County in 2009 of "a very large dirty black man-like creature with his hands around an aspen tree....This was no bear, It was large and shaggy looking." The encounter is remarkably similar to what the miners experienced near Leadville in 1880. The encounter is spurred on by a mysterious howl, and the being is described as a mix between a human and an anomalous hairy creature. Finally, a report from Routt County in 1970 details how hunters sighted a large creature covered in shaggy black hair with "eyes [that] appeared to be intelligent, what I would call a knowing look." In the details of the report on the BFRO website, the hunter explains how they submitted a report to the Colorado State and Game officer, to which the officer replied that it could have only been a bear and that the use of alcohol was prohibited while hunting. This upset the sober hunter, who clarified what he had seen was not a bear; it was between seven and eight feet tall and walked bipedally. These individuals were used to seeing creatures such as bears in the wilderness and were merely reporting what they had seen in the Colorado wilderness.

ETHNOGRAPHIC REPORTS

While the BFRO database is an invaluable resource for someone researching Bigfoot memorates, it can be limited in the sense that the researcher is not getting the reports from the individual involved. Instead, they are mediated through a second party—that is, the BFRO representative who is documenting the narrative. Throughout this book I have used online databases as loci of supernatural legends, but I believe that the method par excellence for documenting memorates is ethnography. Ethnography is a method of research developed largely in the field of anthropology that involves interviewing and participant observation. So in researching for this book, I did my own ethnographic interviewing with individuals in Colorado who have reported to have Bigfoot encounters.

The first person I interviewed is Jim, the owner and manager of The Sasquatch Outpost, a wonderful Bigfoot museum in Bailey, Colorado. The Sasquatch Outpost has become sort of the epicenter of Bigfoot culture in Colorado. Jim is somewhat of a micro-celebrity in the Colorado Bigfoot scene, having appeared in many documentaries and operating his own podcast, *Sasquatch Outpost with Jim Myers*. Bailey is in many ways the "microcosm on the edge of the circle" referenced in the John Keel quote at the beginning of this chapter. Jim appears in a popular YouTube video titled "The Bigfoot of Bailey Colorado and its Portal"; it is the site of the so-called Bigfoot Mystery Film of a supposed Bigfoot taken by a Scout leader in the 1960s; the TV show *Finding Bigfoot* chose Bailey as its filming location for their Colorado episode; and Wellington Lake has a reputation as a hotbed for Bigfoot activity. Jim provided the following description of his encounter:

> *I've had one daytime sighting that would be a Class A when I was fishing at Wellington Lake. Early in the morning I saw something standing on a rock outcropping about two hundred yards above me. It was very tall, all one color, looking down from this rock, and I knew from experience in climbing up there that it was an extremely steep hillside. I had to get up there on my hands and knees. So this thing's looking down and a fish grabbed my fly, and I turned to look at the fish and I looked back and the Bigfoot was gone. I mean it wasn't moving away—it was literally just gone. I can't explain it. But at nighttime I've seen their eyes now I would say definitively at least five or six times, which is a fantastic experience to see something that's eyes are glowing, not reflecting. So again, I can't explain it. Then I've had many encounters, which is what I would call them, where they'll come to my tent at night and push my tent or mess with my tent in some way. Or they'll throw objects at me when I'm in the woods or vocalize in some way. So it's not a sighting, I didn't see them in*

> *those situations, but they wanted me to know that they were there. There's no question about that.*

His narrative is tightly organized and features more "supernatural" elements than a typical BFRO report, as he describes the Bigfoot as disappearing and also chooses to classify it as Bigfoot in no uncertain terms. His narrative conforms to the structure of personal narrative that the linguists William Labov and Joshua Waletzky identified: abstract, orientation, complication, evaluation, resolution and coda. He also uses rhetorical strategies that Elliot Oring says strengthen the believability of supernatural narratives, such as making an assertion that attests to the truth of the narrative (They were there. There's no question about that); and providing a possible explanation (I think there are times they are here physical in flesh and blood, and I think there are times when they move in whatever way they do that, into a different dimension or different sphere that we can't see).[94]

A second individual I interviewed is Chad, who works in banking software, is a member of Colorado's BFRO contingency and goes on

The Sasquatch Outpost in Bailey, Colorado. *Photo by author.*

yearly Bigfoot expeditions with his friends. Chad shared an experience he had in a remote section of the Flat Tops Wilderness Area in northeast Colorado:

> *From right behind that campfire stands up this big figure, that classic kind of Sasquatch outline. And I told my buddy Matt, I said, "Oh man I think I'm looking at one." And then it took off and ran up this hill— of course I didn't hit record. It was real quick—it was four or five seconds. But it ran up this hill, Jack, and you know it was on two legs at first and then it switched to four and it crested this hill. This hill was no joke, like to hike to the top you have to go up a switchback. It crested this thing in three seconds, just amazing.*

Like many Colorado Bigfoot reports, there is a certain amount of ambiguity to Chad's sighting. What he had seen was manifested through a thermal scope, a common technological device that shows heat signatures and is commonly used in the search for Bigfoot. But the time and place of Chad's sighting are, I believe, important to understanding the role of Bigfoot in the modern world. Unlike many of the hunters on the BFRO database who just happened to see a Bigfoot-like creature, Chad and his friends were on an expedition where they were looking for the creature. Some authors have argued that the search for Bigfoot is an extension of the modern search for spiritual and religious meaning, an unmediated experience of the transcendental Mystery.[95] Others have argued that Bigfoot is part of the quest for a connection with the wilderness and nature.[96] In this case, I think it was a little bit of both. Like Jim, Chad expressed a belief that there may be something supernatural about Bigfoot. If that is the case, witnessing such a creature is, in a sense, a religious or spiritual experience. The expedition itself gave Chad and his friends an opportunity to escape into the beauty of nature and to enjoy one another's company. Perhaps that is more valuable than sighting a hitherto documented or understood creature.

A final interview I conducted was with David, a marketing executive from New York who came face-to-face with a Bigfoot-like being near Crater Lake in the San Juan National Forest of Colorado. Jim and his partner would take yearly camping trips from Colorado in order to escape the hustle and bustle of the country's most populated city. The pristine wilderness of Colorado offers a perfect alternative to that lifestyle, until one is staring down a menacing, gigantic, unknown creature:

A view of part of the Flat Tops Wilderness Area from the Ripple Creek Overlook. *Photo by Jeffrey Beall, Wikimedia Commons.*

> *When I turned to look up the trail there was this huge frickin' thing there. It was pitch black, mind you. The only thing I could see were the sides of its face, and its eyes. And I'll never forget those eyes....These things were like completely green; they looked like headlights almost. And it was very tall, and I was looking up at it from where we were.... At first I thought it was a bear, but I realized it was way too tall to be a bear. If it was a bear, it would be a big bear, and it would have to be standing up, and it wasn't moving. It wasn't blinking, nothing. It was just staring at me.*
>
> *And then I noticed there was another set of eyes behind it that suddenly appeared out of nowhere. And I knew it was behind it, and I could see it was doing like a figure eight. It's hard to explain, but a smaller set of eyes were probably halfway down this thing, and you could see between its legs because sometimes the eyes would disappear and you could see that it was going between something. So it would go, as you're staring at it, from the right side to the left side, in a figure eight, like in an infinity loop kind of motion, right? So I knew it was on two legs if that makes sense. And immediately I knew what it was....*

> *And then I got terrified, I go, "Shit it has a baby." So I couldn't really speak, I was mumbling something.... I think I blurted out "Bigfoot."... The thing looked down, it blinked, and then it turned and walked down the trail.*

David's narrative is full of idiosyncratic details, such as the eyes looking like headlights and figure eight movement of the younger creature between the legs of the adult. Unlike Jim and Chad, David was mere feet away from the being, albeit during the dead of night. Jim and Chad also expressed a belief that Bigfoot may be in some way supernatural, while David did not. For David, this was a terrifying encounter with a huge, unknown animal that was lurking outside his tent in the wilderness. But this experience can in a certain sense be read as a symbol of what it was David was searching for in the Colorado wilderness: a direct experience of the mysteries of the outdoors, the hope that there is something still out there as of yet unidentified by the technologies and machinations of the city.

CONCLUSION

I am not here to tell you whether or not these individuals sighted Bigfoot or not. That is the role of a cryptozoologist, among whose ranks I don't count myself. Instead, as a folklorist, I see my job as documenting and researching these reports, hoping to interpret them and not starting from a position of disbelief. Too often scholars start from a position of assuming they know how the world works, and in the case of Bigfoot memorates, I think it is disrespectful and dismissive at best and ethnocentric at worst to tell a person that what they saw was not Bigfoot. As Hufford made clear, stories about hairy humanoids are quite ancient and traditions about

The author at The Sasquatch Outpost. *Photo by author.*

them incredibly stable, and the narratives documented herein are consistent with that tradition.

The history of reports about these hairy humanoids in Colorado dates to at least the 1880s. Colorado has been the site of hundreds of reported sightings of Bigfoot according to the BFRO database, with the oldest report coming in the 1920s. Sightings continue to be reported to the current day, and videos such as the one from the Narrow Gauge Railroad mentioned at the beginning of the chapter carry on the tradition of ambiguity started by the Patterson-Gimlin Film nearly sixty years ago at the time of this writing. To end this essay how I started it, I'll state Hufford's observation, which I have found to be most useful:

> *As soon as we become truly careful about our logic and our understanding of our own assumptive sets we shall be able to begin to work seriously with a huge body of material of great importance within our culture, and to do so in ways that promise a variety of very exciting possibilities.*[97]

3

HERE BE DRAGONS

LAKE MONSTERS IN COLORADO

Beware deep waters that hold old secrets.
—*The War of the Rohirrim*

For most people, the words *lake monster* inevitably conjure images of the Loch Ness Monster, the reigning poster child for legendary aquatic beasts. What they may not realize, however, is that Loch Ness is by no means the only lake reputed to be the home to some as-of-yet unidentified saurian creature. Every state in the United States has at least one lake monster, and traditions of these cryptids—creatures reputed to exist in folklore and legend but not yet recognized by science—can be found all over the planet. The Loch Ness Monster legends date to the seventh century AD, when Saint Columba was said to have placated a water beast by making the sign of the cross. This, like many other Catholic monster-slaying narratives, can be read as a thinly veiled allegory for the conversion of local Pagans, but folklore about aquatic and draconic monsters may have been based off of even older traditions such as those of kelpies or the lesser-known Caortannach and Oilliphéist.

Throughout history, there has been an apparent obsession with monsters that inhabit the world's seas, lakes and oceans. The Greek historian Herodotus wrote about a Persian military commander's ships being destroyed and his men devoured by sea monsters.[98] Behemoth and Leviathan figure heavily in the biblical book of Job. Eighteenth-century maps depict sea monsters and other fantastical creatures at the limits of civilization, and legends of the kraken may owe their origins to the rare but "real" giant squid.[99] North America is full of such legends, including Ogopogo at Lake Okanagan in British Columbia, Champ from Lake Champlain, the Bear Lake Monster on the border of Idaho and Utah and even the hyperlocal Lake Lieberman Monster, a consciously fabricated legend at Binghamton University that makes its home in a drainage ditch.[100] Many North American lake monsters draw directly from their legendary predecessor Nessie, including Lake Erie's Bessie, Chesapeake Bay's Chessie, Crescent Lake's Cressie, Lake Superior's Pressie and Lake Tahoe's Tahoe Tessy.

It should come to no surprise, then, that Colorado is home to its own lake monsters. Our own Nessie spin-off is Essie, the Lake Estes Monster.[101] In my research, I have been able to locate ten lakes in Colorado with their own legends about lake monsters, though I am fairly confident that through ethnographic research it is likely more can be identified. Much of the popular literature about lake monsters comes from either skeptics hoping to debunk lake monster legends in favor of explanations such as logs, misidentified known lake-dwellers or tricks of light or from cryptozoologists trying to prove that these lakes are inhabited by strange or anomalous creatures. Instead, as a folklorist I am motivated by the simple but endlessly complicated question: Why? Why do we make legends about lake monsters? Why are these particular lakes associated with legendary monsters? To be certain, there can be experiential sources for such legends. People do often report having anomalous sightings at lakes, but I believe that if we plunge below the surface of these legends, important insights into the connections between lakes and monsters can be revealed.

So why are lakes the sites of legends? The folklorist Lisa Gabbert, in her work on Sharlie, a lake monster from Payette Lake in Idaho, suggests that one reason is that "mysterious qualities are commonly attributed to bodies of water in which monsters are presumed to reside."[102] In other words, the particular lakes that monsters are associated with are often part of a larger legend complex. These legends and rumors include stories of the lake being bottomless or being the sites of underwater caves or even tunnels connecting them to other lakes.[103] This is precisely the case in Colorado, where the Twin Lakes Serpent is said to hide in grottos and even travel through tunnels connecting it to Cottonwood Lake. Historically, the Twin Lakes Serpent is probably Colorado's most famous lake monster, but it is also tied to another key aspect of lake monster legends Gabbert identifies: boosterism, the endeavor to promote the legend for financial gain. The Twin Lakes Serpent was likely a fabrication by the controversial "spinner of yarn" Orth Stein,

Lake Estes, Colorado, photo by Sarbjit Bahga on *Wikimedia Commons*.

who, while editor of the *Leadville Herald*, published a series of articles about the creature in the late 1800s. Those same articles led the ownership at the Interlaken Resort, a ritzy destination at Twin Lakes, to attempt to capitalize on the legend to increase their sales. But this touristic and voyeuristic aspect of the lake monster is also key to understanding their popularity, because as a monster mediating boundaries between the real and the "unreal," they are also able to mediate the fluid relationship between insiders and outsiders, or tourist and non-tourist, at places like the Interlaken Resort.

There is something beyond rumors of caves and tunnels or the touristic element of lake monsters that make them fascinating, though. Water itself is a mystery. I, for one, find myself, while standing on the precipice of a body of water, both fascinated and terrified by what lies beneath the surface. Author Colin Dickey elaborates on this point, saying:

> *Above the surface, we presume complete control over lakes: waterways for commerce, the transportation of goods, recreation, and sports. But the murky depths remain unknown, a foreign terrain. To see a strange animal breaking the surface of a lake is to feel the eerie presence of another realm breaking through, from the unknowable world below, troubling our serene understanding of water.*[104]

Dickey cites Mark Fisher, the greatest hauntologist since founder Jacques Derrida, who highlights this key term, *eerie*, as "the feeling of there being presence where there should be absence, or absence where there should be presence."[105] Perhaps this is precisely why lake monsters are so ubiquitous. Water is eerie in the Fisherian sense of the word. These lakes shouldn't be home to plesiosaurs, and yet, the legends suggest otherwise. Dickey also says that lakes are part of our everyday life, in that they are not remote or exotic. But I would suggest the opposite. The lakes in Colorado that are associated with legends aren't always the ones that are the closest, nor are they the farthest. They are the ones that are just far enough to be considered a journey to get to. In other words, they lie in the liminal space between the exotic and the ordinary, and that is the perfect place for a legend.

THE TWIN LAKES MONSTER

By far the most famous lake monster in Colorado, or at least the state's most consequential, is the Twin Lakes Monster. In 1884, a series of articles appeared in Leadville's *Carbonate Chronicle* that detailed how the lake was said to be inhabited by a strange creature that was described as being upward of thirty feet long, with a head like an owl, a pronged tail and spikes down its back. The articles, however, were written by Orth Stein, an editor for the paper who would later be remembered as a teller of tall tales, whose life spiraled downward amid accusations of murder.[106]

The Twin Lakes Monster is a perfect example of how aquatic monsters become embroiled in boosterism and commercialization and are said to inhabit lakes that are associated with other legends. It seems that from the very beginning, Stein's articles were fabrications to increase readership in the Leadville papers. By the 1890s, an entrepreneur named Billy Passmore had opened a resort called The Interlaken, where he tried to capitalize on the popularity of the monster.[107] Crucially, the Twin Lakes are said to have underground tunnels that connect them to other lakes such as Cottonwood Lake, and the monster hides in strange underground caverns.

The first article about the Twin Lakes Serpent appeared in the June 28, 1884 edition of the *Carbonate Chronicle* with the title "A Hideous Visitor":

> *Planted on the crest of the range by some marvelous freak of nature that has puzzled every geologist since their discovery, without a known outlet large enough to account for their limpid clearness and purity, of unknown depth and unexplored subterranean contour, these lakes themselves are a mystery so profound that one not unnaturally looks for the strange and abnormal*

in connection with them.... Yesterday morning James Powell, a miner and prospector, who lives close to the Twin Lakes house, was walking with a party of several....

As they looked they were appalled and bewildered to see a GIGANTIC HEAD rise from the surface. They stood petrified with amazement and terror as a neck fully twenty feet long reared itself out of the waters and poised there for a moment. The contour of the monster was that of a colossal serpent. The head was long and pointed, and a dull olive in color, with a gigantic mouth and dark round eyes. Its skin was apparently perfectly smooth, like that of a cat-fish or trout, and the monstrous body was of a diameter fully as large, if not larger, than the head....

Twin Lakes, largest lakes in the Rockies, *Library of Congress.*

> *This is not the first time that a subterranean monster has been connected with the lakes. There has been a tradition older than the oldest inhabitant, and coming from a source so remote that no one could trace its origin, that they contained on unknown creature of colossal size and terrible appearance, that had risen at intervals of years and terrified the chance explorers who had beheld it. Where this story arose that was handed down by the natives and had become one of the legends of the place was a mystery that the appearance of yesterday may go a great ways toward unraveling.*
>
> *The theory has been sustained by many scientists who have visited the lakes, that beneath the bodies of water upon the surface, there are a series of subterranean ones, and probably a river as well, that feed them and keep them pure. The volcanic origin of that portion of the mountain and the porous quality of the lime rock that form its basis are INDICATIVE OF CAVERNS and the fact that no sounding line ever yet brought to the lake has succeeded In touching the bottom is another suggestive fact.*[108]

Remarkably, many of the same attributes that are given to lakes in the twenty-first century that are associated with lake monsters were being articulated in this news article from the 1880s. The lake is said to be mysterious, a geologic anomaly that has unknown depths, "a mystery so profound that one not unnaturally looks for the strange and abnormal in connection with them." Like the Loch Ness Monster, the creature makes a sudden appearance to unsuspecting visitors, who Stein seems to have invented, and then disappears into the lake's unknown depths, which are home to both underground caves, tunnels and even other hidden bodies of water. The author even gives an explanation for what the creature may be, citing the possibility of a prehistoric creature that somehow escaped extinction as the answer. Such speculation is also true for the Loch Ness Monster, which some theorize is a plesiosaur that migrates to the lake through river passages that connect it to the sea.

Several weeks later, Stein wrote a follow-up to "A Hideous Visitor," an article titled "Down in the Depths," which appeared in the July 12, 1884 edition of the *Carbonate Chronicle*. The article details how Professor J.L. Godat of the Smithsonian, Professor James Winter and Dr. Ellba White visited Twin Lakes after having read the original article as part of a government commission to explore the Rocky Mountains. The problem, however, is that it seems that these individuals never existed. I could find no record of a J.L. Godat from the Smithsonian, nor was there any discernible Professor Winter or Dr. White. The timeline doesn't add up either, as these individuals would have had to make the trip to Leadville extremely quickly after the original article appeared. I can only conclude, then, that the story from this article was part of the web of yarn that Stein was spinning. He indicates this in the article, saying in a tongue-in-cheek fashion about the supposed letter he had received from Godat that "its authenticity and the correctness of its statements are not vouched for by the Chronicle."[109]

The supposed letter that Stein had received from this seemingly imaginary group of explorers detailed how they used a submarine called the "Intelligent Whale" that Godat named the *Naiad* to explore the depths of Twin Lakes. While underwater, they saw a number of strange creatures, many of which emerged from caves and caverns. One of the creatures "had but one fin that appeared to the eye, a large one on its back, although there must have been others glued to its side," while another "was nearer a species of swordfish than anything else, with a sharp-looking tusk protruding from its snout, the length of the creature being about three feet," and there were also "water snakes, which appeared under the lurid gleam of the light to be all sorts of fantastic colors, green predominating." By far the strangest creature Godat

Twin Lakes with Mount Elbert in the background, *Library of Congress.*

described was "a sea spider… with innumerable legs that were constantly stretched out and withdrawn in their hunt for prey."[110]

Reading Stein's articles is like reading a Thomas Pynchon novel. They are full of impossible stories full of compelling, mysterious characters on clandestine missions. I am inclined to interpret the entire Twin Lakes Serpent saga as being one of his famous tall tales. These stories are ambiguous. Especially from our temporal distance, it is difficult to tell if there really ever was a J.L. Godat. I, for one, have not been able to verify his existence. True or not, Stein's articles are prime examples of the legend genre precisely because of their ambiguity. The legends also led to action, as people traveled to the Interlaken in hopes to catch a glimpse of the legendary serpent. And the method of creating a lake monster legend to create attention from a popular audience that Stein established in Colorado has been replicated ever since.

THE COTTONWOOD SEA SERPENT

The connection between lake monsters and the lakes they inhabit being home to other mysterious phenomena such as hidden tunnels is crucial to understanding how lake monster legends operate and why they are sustained. Clearly this is the case with the Twin Lakes Serpent, but it also connects it to another famous Colorado lake monster: the Cottonwood Sea Serpent, also known as "Diabello Dinothesium," which translates (roughly) to "devil dinosaur." As the name indicates, this creature makes its legendary home at Cottonwood Lake, a relatively small lake outside of Buena Vista and, like the Twin Lakes Serpent, is said to travel through hidden tunnels to other lakes in Colorado and as far as Japan.

The original story about the Cottonwood Sea Serpent appeared in the August 22, 1907 edition of the *Colorado Republican* in an article titled "What the Cottonwood Sea Serpent Story Really Is." Like the Twin Lakes Serpent, the Cottonwood Sea Serpent is said to make "annual visits in August and September."[111] The anonymous subscriber who wrote this article said, like Stein, that he got his information from "two men well known for their skill and deep research" who "made a full and complete investigation, the report of which has been kept a secret up to this time, and now it is given to the public."[112] The author connects this sea serpent to older legends, saying, "It is a gigantic herbivorous aquatic animal. The ancient Greeks called it the Terrible

Monster."[113] This is presumably in reference to Typhon, the serpentine, giant son of Gaia and Tartarus who fought Zeus for cosmic supremacy and, with the equally monstrous Echidna, sired many terrifying creatures, including the three-headed dog Cerberus, the Lernean Hydra and Ladon, the dragon tasked with guarding the golden apples in the Garden of the Hesperides.

But besides having classical provenance, the Cottonwood Sea Serpent also traveled through hidden chambers, much like the Twin Lakes Serpent or even the Hogwarts basilisk. The monster makes its appearance in Cottonwood Lake each year to do "its annual assessment work in opening up the subterranean passages between this country and Japan; possibly enlarging them with a view for the use of submarines."[114] In fact, the Cottonwood Sea Serpent and the Twin Lakes Serpent may be one in the same because "as to the underground connections and that the Diabello is seen in other lakes, assures us that there are connections."[115] The article intimates that the monster recently caused a geomythical rise in the lake's surface, which "was caused by the choking up of the underground outlet. There seems to be no question but that this monster was the plug and become wedged in for a time prior to his appearance in Cottonwood lake."[116] With its connections to classical mythology and a mysterious underground system of tunnels connecting it to other lakes across both the state and the planet, the Cottonwood Sea Serpent is a prime example of how Colorado's legends connect it to a wider tradition of folklore.

THE STANDLEY LAKE MONSTER

The Standley Lake Monster is generally depicted looking like a giant squid, with long tentacles and a bulbous head. It is reminiscent of the Kraken, the legends of which are based on sightings of the giant squid. This is opposed to the Dillon Reservoir cutout, which looks (shockingly) like Nessie. Like the previous lake monsters covered, however, the Standley Lake Monster is also a hoax, created by the Westminster creative offices to encourage people to go to the lake.

On July 20, 2016, a Facebook page called "Westminster Enquirer," fashioning itself as "Westminster's MOST reliable news source," posted a grainy picture that appeared to show the head of a large creature cresting the surface of Standley Lake. The picture was accompanied by the caption:

> *Residents report unusual sightings at Standley Lake Regional Park. Others dismiss reports, citing over-sized pelicans as a possible explanation. City of Westminster Parks, Recreation & Libraries has not commented on the wild claims. Leave a comment if you have seen anything strange at the lake.*[117]

The photo is similar to the "surgeon's photograph," the famous photo allegedly taken of the Loch Ness Monster by Robert Kenneth Wilson in 1934, which is generally understood to be a hoax. However, there is no doubt that the photo of the Standley Lake Monster that appeared on the Westminster Enquirer Facebook page is a hoax.

I've often said that if I worked for a chamber of commerce or a city's marketing department, the first thing I would do is invent a monster to drive

The Standley Monster poster. *Photo by author.*

tourism to the area. Across the country, local monsters spark interest in areas that might be otherwise overlooked. Such is the case for Mothman, the Flatwoods Monster, Wisconsin's Hodag and, perhaps most appropriately, the Loch Ness Monster. Standley Lake is by no means a place that might be overlooked; it is a beautiful lake half an hour from the heart of Denver. Nonetheless, the creation of a monster from the lake is one of the first things Rich Neumann and his marketing team did when he started as the marketing supervisor for the city's parks, recreation and libraries department.[118]

The photograph from the *Westminster Enquirer* sparked debate over its veracity, but an article ran in *The Denver Post* explaining that the Facebook page and the legend were created by the marketing team in order to get people to the lake. The monster they created is imaginative and detailed. It hibernates during the winter, which is no surprise given Colorado's winter climates, but during its active seasons in the spring and winter, intrepid explorers can find multicolored eggs and even rainbow poop, which are both specifically meant for children so that they may be excited to visit the lake.[119] While the Standley Lake Monster was a folkloresque creation by the city's marketing department, it is in line with the tendency in Colorado history to use monsters as a way to draw visitors to the state's many lakes.

LAKE KATHERINE MONSTER

At this point, you may be wondering if there are any lake monsters in Colorado that are not easily dismissed as outright hoaxes. The answer to that is yes: the Lake Katherine Monster. An article in the October 25, 1979 edition of *The Aspen Times* titled "'Monster Reported at Lake Katherine" details an encounter that two fishermen had at the remote Lake Katherine:

> *Something odd was swimming around in Lake Katherine the night of Aug 25. Jerry Cross of the Environmental Protection Agency and his father-in-law, Bill Hoppe, went to Lake Katherine in the Mt Zirkel Wilderness Area west of Walden for a weekend of fishing. On the second night, they were fishing from the shore with a pair of Coleman lanterns. According to Cross, the fishing was good under a clear, moonless sky when suddenly the fish stopped biting and everything became quiet. Cross said he looked out onto the lake and saw something moving across the surface of the water. When the thing came near the lights, Cross*

View of the West face of Mount Zirkel. *Photo by Tom Konrad on Wikimedia Commons.*

Distant view of Dillon Reservoir, near Frisco. *Library of Congress.*

> *said he saw eyes, three inches in diameter, reflecting the light of his lantern. He estimated the creature to be about 15–20 feet long with a hump on its back sticking out of the water about three feet. Speculation on the identity of the creature is inconclusive and ranges from an elk or moose to a swimming beaver to something unknown. Cross claims he got a good enough look at the creature to be sure it wasn't an animal he had ever seen before. The lake itself is something of an enigma. Lake Katherine sits at 10,000 feet and has been measured at 115 feet deep in one place, while the bottom has never been found in other places. Last year, divers sent into the lake to look for the body of a fisherman described the lake as "the weirdest place they had ever dived."*[120]

The sighting of Cross and Hoppe can be classified as a type of supernatural, anomalous or fringe encounter that is generated by experience. Lake Katherine is remote. The Zirkel wilderness is one of the more difficult places to reach in the state. As opposed to Standley Lake, which is in a fairly well-populated area, Lake Katherine is beyond the limens of society. It's not necessarily the type of place you would want to market to tourists, such as Twin Lakes or the Dillon Reservoir.

Interestingly, the article mentions that "the lake itself is something of an enigma." It conforms with Gabbert's observation that lakes with monster legends are often rumored to be bottomless, as the article says that "the bottom has never been found in other places," and that it has been described by divers as "the weirdest place they had ever dived." While the article does provide possible naturalistic explanations for the creature, this remains one of the most intriguing unsolved lake mysteries of Colorado.

THE GRAND LAKE SEA-SERPENT

A final Colorado lake monster for this chapter is an enigmatic one: the Grand Lake Sea-Serpent. As has been my modus operandi for the chapter, this legend comes from yet another historic newspaper, in this case an article titled "Grand Lake Sea-Serpent" in the September 17, 1885 edition of the *Georgetown Courier*. The article describes how the proprietors of "Taylor's museum" enlisted a man in Grand Lake to "capture the monster of that region."[121] However, the article doesn't provide any other details of what that monster is, and it seems that they are expecting the audience to already be familiar with the legend. Unfortunately, no other articles exist to elaborate on this nineteenth-century story. The man they had enlisted was not successful in finding the monster and, instead, sent them a small worm.

According to the Grand Lake Area Historical Society, however, the lake has been associated with legends since the mid-1800s.[122] One of the first white settlers of the lake, Joseph L. Wescott, was told a story by a Ute chief about how the lake is "haunted ground" and that his ancestors had once fought an army of "phantom warriors" there.[123] Like many of the other lake monsters covered, their legends are associated with a place already rumored to be strange or haunted.

Top: Town of Grand Lake. *Library of Congress.*

Bottom: Grand Lake, just outside of Rocky Mountain National Park. *Photo by Carol M. Highsmith on Wikimedia Commons.*

CONCLUSION

With over 1,500 publicly owned lakes in the state,[124] Colorado is bound to have its share of lake monster legends. While this chapter has been fairly comprehensive, there are several lake monsters I've omitted for lack of data, including the Mud Lake Monster, the Loch Lomond Monster and the Horsetooth Reservoir Monster. Lakes are mysterious. They are both near and far. Their depths are both enticing and terrifying. They draw the observer in, making them question what unknown creatures might lurk within. Often lakes with monster legends are said to have underground caves or tunnels, such as Twin Lakes. They might be rumored to be bottomless, or just plain weird, like Lake Katherine. They could be associated with other supernatural legends, as is the case with Grand Lake. Lake monsters are often used as tourist attractions and are used to get visitors to look for signs of their legendary inhabitants, like the Standley Monster. So next time you are out at one of Colorado's many lakes, keep your eyes open, because you never know when you will see something unexplainable, like what happened to Jerry Cross and Bill Hoppe on that fateful day in 1979.

4

KNOCK, KNOCK, WHO'S THERE? COLORADO'S TOMMYKNOCKERS

Faerie is a perilous land, and in it are pitfalls for the unwary and dungeons for the overbold.
—J.R.R. Tolkien

Folklore is a shapeshifter that takes on new forms to fit new contexts. One of the greatest examples of this in Colorado are the Tommyknockers, elf-like spirits said to inhabit the state's mines. The Tommyknockers originated in Cornwall, a county in England, and are related to a great number of other gnome-like entities in European folklore. In Europe, there is a rich tradition of gnomes, which are on the whole diminutive spirits that inhabit underground spaces, tasked with guarding treasures. Ronald James, a folklorist who has researched the transformation of knockers, as they are called in Cornwall, to Tommyknockers, as they became known in the American West, notes that in Germany they are known as Kobolde or Wichtlein and as Coblynau among the Welsh.[125] The knockers are spirits that inhabit mines and are generally thought to be morally ambiguous. James describes them in the following terms: "[These] supernatural beings were regarded as dwarf-like men with wrinkled faces and long gray beards. Taking their name from the background noise of rapping and tapping were mischievous creatures. If treated kindly, however, they could be helpful."[126]

One of the first folklorists to document traditions about knockers in Cornwall was William Bottrell, who included fieldwork he did on the topic in his *Traditions and Hearthside Stories of West Cornwall*, first published in 1873.

Bottrell includes a conversation he had with a man named "Uncle Bill" who said that they believe in "sperats" that they call "knackers." Uncle Bill told the story of his friend Tom Trevorrow (in typical friend-of-a-friend fashion), who had upset the knockers and incurred their malevolent side. Tom had taken up work at a mine, or *bal* as it was called in the Cornish vernacular, that was known to be haunted by knockers. Day after day, Tom heard the knockers working the mines. The knocks from their picks, from which their name is derived, became louder and more intolerable as they moved closer to him. Finally, he had enough, and cried out, "Go to blazes, you cussed old Jews' sperrats; or I'll scat your brains out." After saying that, stones fell on him, but still he resolved to work in the morning. Tom took a break to eat and heard the voices of the knockers cry out to him, saying:

Tom Trevorrow! Tom Trevorrow!
Leave some of thy fuggan for Bucca,
Or bad luck to thee, to-morrow!

Tommy Trevorrow, Tommy Trevorrow!
We'll send thee bad luck to-morrow,
Thou old curmudgeon, to eat all thy fuggan,
And not leave a didjan for Bucca![127]

Tom went back to work the next day, scared by the knockers' warnings, but his decision to not give them any food (*fuggan*) proved to be a mistake. The floor of the mine he was working in caved in, and he narrowly escaped, but it took his mining tools with it. After losing his tools and the portion of the mine he was working in, his bad luck followed him until he finally had to leave Ballowal, the cursed mine of the knockers.

I preface this introduction to the nature of knockers, later known in America as Tommyknockers, with the story of Tom Trevorrow because it underscores several key aspects of what these beings are in folkloric tradition. First is the belief that knockers are the spirits of Jewish miners. This can be seen through Tom's admonishment of the picking sounds (which indicate the presence of knockers) as "cussed old Jews' sperrats." This notion can be seen elsewhere in literature from the nineteenth century. For example, in Charles Kingsley's *Yeast: A Problem*, his character Tregarva goes through a harrowing journey in the mines and eventually "heard the knockers knocking." Sir Lancelot, whom Tregarva has just narrated his story to, asks who the knockers are, to which Tregarva replies, "They are ghosts, the miners hold, of the old Jews, sir, that crucified our Lord, and were sent for slaves by the Roman emperors to work the mines."[128]

It was thought that the knockers did not work on the Sabbath because of their nature as Jewish ghosts.[129] An excerpt from the mineralogist and antiquarian Robert Hunt in his 1908 *Popular Romances of the West of England* complicates that, however. Hunt says:

> *The buccas or knockers are believed to inhabit the rocks, caves, adits, and wells of Cornwall....There was a well where those industrious small people might every day be heard busy at their labours—digging with pickaxe and shovel....On Christmas-day—on the Jews' Sabbath—on Easter day—and on All Saints' Day—no work was done.*[130]

The knockers' interconnection with other fairy and elf-like beings in European folklore makes giving one catch-all definition of what they are difficult. While they are thought to be the ghosts of Jewish miners in Cornwall, they also act like and are similar to elves, and more broadly to the Sidhe, the aboveground fairies of Ireland.[131] Folklore transforms for new contexts, and as we see throughout this chapter, the knocker changed its form and nature to meet new context as they moved from Cornwall to America.

Another characteristic that Tom Trevorrow's story tells us about knockers is that they will punish those who treat them poorly and reward good behavior. Because Tom curses them and, more importantly, does not placate them by leaving them food, the knockers react negatively and he is not able to keep mining in the places that they are active. Hunt cites a specific mine, Ransom Mine, and its accompanying legends that display this dichotomy. In Hunt's story, a man and his son saw knockers bringing up some "shining ore." The man and his son struck a deal with the knockers, saying if they could mine the ore for the good folk, they'd give the knockers one-tenth of the profits. The old man always kept his deal, but when he died, the son became greedy and did not pay. Because of his greed, the lode failed, and he died broke and drunk.[132] When the man and his son helped the knockers, they came upon riches, but once they broke the deal, it led to their downfall. Importantly, this knocker story warns against greed, a trait that no longer was present in the American Tommyknocker, which is a culture that values capitalistic ambition.[133]

Should we consider the knocker a monster? This simple question does not have a straightforward answer. As David Puglia observes, defining monsters is inherently difficult, and authors are almost bound to disagree with one universal definition.[134] Yet we can look at the root of the word *monster* for clues about how they operate. Monster comes from the Latin *monstrum*, rooted in *monere*, meaning "to warn, to portend."[135] The knocker serves as a warning about what can happen to miners—in the Cornish context, for overstepping their boundaries and becoming greedy. Literal belief in knockers was extremely prevalent, however, so breaking down their metaphorical aspects is overly simplistic. Like other monsters and creatures from folk tradition to be covered in this book, the knockers operate on several layers of meaning, often simultaneously. They can be metaphors in which cultural fears and anxieties about uncanny, liminal spaces such as the mine are inscribed; they can be figures of literal belief; and finally, especially in America and particularly in Colorado, they can become local mascots and figures of industry.

TOMMYKNOCKERS IN COLORADO

When the Cornish immigrated to America, they brought their folk beliefs about knockers as well as their mining expertise. Naturally, with the mining boom in the American West, the Cornish began to populate those regions. By the 1860s, the "Cousin Jacks," as these Cornish miners were called, had started working the mines in Colorado.[136] During the course of the Cornish diffusion across the country, the knocker took on a new name, the Tommyknocker. The Swedish folklorist Carl von Sydow describes in his work how during cultural migration, aspects of folklore are retained.[137] The knocker was evidently one of the aspects of Cornish lore that was important enough to retain. But during this process of moving to a new place and a new context, aspects of this folkloric being changed. In Colorado, the Tommyknocker is conceived of as a morally ambiguous subterranean mining spirit. Instead of being thought of as the ghosts of dead Jewish miners, in Colorado and the West they are thought of as the spirits of dead miners from the particular mines they occupy.[138]

The study of Tommyknockers has a fairly straightforward genealogy, as far as who has studied them academically and in the field. The folklorist Wayland Hand did extensive work on Tommyknocker traditions in Montana, Utah and Nevada during the 1940s. His work documented how similar beliefs in the Tommyknockers migrated to these Western mines. For example, he details that in California the Tommyknockers were so named because of the knocking sounds they make and that clay effigies were often left for them as good luck.[139] In Utah, he was informed that if a miner were to follow those sounds between midnight and two o'clock in the morning, they would strike it rich.[140]

In Colorado, no one has done more extensive work on Tommyknockers than Caroline Bancroft. Bancroft came from an affluent Colorado family, and her father, Dr. F.J. Bancroft, was the founder of the Colorado Historical Society. She continued her family's legacy of historical work by writing books on topics like Colorado's ghost towns, lost gold mines and the infamous Baby Doe Tabor. In 1945, she published her influential article "Folklore of the Central City District, Colorado." The article featured fieldwork she did in what she called the "Central City District," which comprises the towns of Blackhawk, Mountain City, Central City and Nevadaville.[141]

The area that Bancroft calls the Central City District was extremely influential during the years between roughly 1859 and 1880 due to its connection with the Colorado gold rush. This area, and Central City in particular, was more influential than the burgeoning capital city of Denver.[142] Bancroft's work in the area included terms used by the Cousin Jacks, including the "Tommy-knockers," which she defined as "gnomes who inhabit the mines."[143]

During the time that Bancroft and Hand were documenting folk belief among these Western mining communities, they noted that literal belief in the Tommyknockers was disappearing. Bancroft included the folk expression "Tommy-knockers are working again" as a colloquialism that was used in these communities. She remarks, however, that "this expression is still heard, but I could find no evidence in the district of any real belief in their existence among the younger men and only fragmentary evidence among the older."[144] Hand documented a similar process in Utah, saying "the belief in spirits of dead men or of ghost-like characters, man or beast, in the mines is not so prevalent as it used to be," and that "legends and superstitions are often based on faulty vision or hearing, or upon a misconstruction of some phenomenon validly observed."[145]

One story Bancroft documented that seems to conform to this explanation of Tommyknocker belief came from a man named Fred de Mandel. The following is the story as Bancroft recounted it:

> *In the Perigo mine, over the hill from Apex, there was a belief that the spirit of John Q.A. Rollins (after whom Rollinsville in Gilpin County is named) was haunting the mine. His ghost was supposed to have been there for*

Above: The Argo Gold Mine. *Photo by Carol M. Highsmith, Library of Congress.*

Opposite, top: Argo Mine close-up. *Photo by Mike Renlund, Flikr CC BY 2.0.*

Opposite, bottom: Water flowing from old mine. *Photo by Craig Talbert, Flikr CC BY 2.0.*

> *some time and every so often the miners would leave their jobs. De Mandel decided to investigate for himself. The mine had been worked at various different periods and on one occasion No. 9 stope had been mucked out but not trammed. De Mandel could hear "pick, pick, pick" and then a pause, in the exact sound and rhythm of a man using a pickax and resting. "If you could have heard it, you'd understand how the idea of tommy-knockers got started. I'd have sworn it was a real miner!" said de Mandel. He finally climbed over all the banks of muck and behind the piles, found a dinner pail with water dropping on it in just that rhythm.*[146]

This anecdote, as told by Bancroft, has several notable features to it. The first of which is that the Tommyknockers were, during the time of de Mandel, conceived of as the spirits of former miners. No longer were these chthonic beings held to be the ghosts of Jewish miners, which is an idea that would not have resonated in the American West as it did for centuries in Cornwall. As Ronald James notes, this change, along with the transformation away from associations with European piskies, meant that the Tommyknockers were becoming unique American (and in this case Colorado) folklore.[147]

ARGO
GOLD MINE & MILL

TUNNEL

A second notable feature of this anecdote is the connection between the geological processes of the mine and supernatural folk belief, which can be considered an example of "geomythology." The geologist Dorothy Vitaliano developed the theory of "geomythology," which she defined as "the real geologic event underlying a myth or legend to which it has given rise."[148] Vitaliano's work is full of fascinating examples of the interconnections between myths and geology, such as the role of volcanic explosions in Icelandic adoption of Christianity over the old Norse gods and geologic explanations for Devil's Tower in Wyoming. We see through the story of Fred de Mandel that ultimately the geological processes were the "real geologic event" that he was interpreting as the presence of the Tommyknockers. Determining the origin of folklore is a fool's errand; this is not to suggest that geological processes are the ultimate explanation of Tommyknocker lore. What this does suggest, however, is that the geological processes of the mines and stories about the Tommyknockers were interwoven.

A third notable feature of Fred de Mandel's account of his Tommyknocker lore is that it is tied to a specific place: the Perigo mine. David Puglia notes that monsters are often "hyperlocal," in that folklore about these creatures operate on specific local levels and contexts.[149] Although the Tommyknocker has roots in Cornwall and has gone through a process of diffusion in America and the American West, this narrative ties these stories to a specific place in Colorado.

In this instance, it is important to note that the Tommyknocker was conceived of as being the ghost of a prospector who used to work at the mines, John Q.A. Rollins. No longer are these "knockers" thought of as ghosts of Jewish miners but rather specific miners who used to work in the mines. Thus, a significant transition has occurred in folkloric beliefs about the nature of these chthonic entities. Ronald James argues that this transition is due to the differences between Cornish and American culture, noting that stories about the spirits of Roman-era Jews were not only unlikely to be culturally relevant but also a historical impossibility. In America, however, belief in ghosts was prevalent.[150] This change in folklore reveals the changing attitudes about Tommyknockers and their spectral nature.

This focus on death also demonstrates realities of the miner's working environment. Working in the mines is an inherently dangerous endeavor. The realm in which these miners work is a liminal zone where the threats of death and disease are always lurking. Improper conditions may lead to cave-ins, and diseases were common among miners. It is not surprising that miners populated their working environment with uncanny characters that had the control over life and death that they perhaps did not. Taking this a step further, there were precarious material realities to the miner's lives. They work in these environments with the hopes of striking it rich. Tommyknockers had not only the power to create or prevent disasters but also the knowledge of where the mine's riches lay.

The story of John Q.A. Rollins haunting the Perigo mine was not idiosyncratic. Bancroft's fieldwork uncovered similar folk beliefs about Tommyknockers in other mines of the Central City District. For example, she details how a foreman at the Chain-O-Mines described two miners quitting their jobs because Tommyknockers were "keeping a cow in there." Bancroft explains that this phrase was used because a sound was coming from the bowels of the earth that sounded like a cow mooing. The foreman investigated and determined that this sound was caused by water dropping onto a tin sheet and reverberating, causing a sound that resembled a cow's moo. Despite this, the miners would not go investigate.[151]

The miners quitting their jobs because of these uncanny sounds that they believed to be caused by Tommyknockers is an example of what folklorists refer to as "ostension." Ostension is used in linguistics to describe "communication via the showing or demonstrating of something directly, as opposed to referring to or representing it indirectly."[152] For example, you may point to an object you want passed to you instead of using audible language to do so. In folkloristics, this term has been used to describe the physical acting out of a legend rather than the mere recitation of it since Linda Dégh and Andrew Vázsonyi's seminal 1983 article "Does the Word 'Dog' Bite? Ostensive Action: A Means of Legend-Telling." Dégh and Vázsonyi looked at how legends like razors in Halloween candy caused people to act ostensively by choosing not to purchase certain candies or go trick-or-treating.[153]

Jeffrey Tolbert and Ian Brodie note that "in folkloric ostension, people ostend the content of a narrative by attempting to experience or witness it for themselves."[154] The foreman's choice of investigating the sound that was tied in legend to Tommyknockers is an act of ostension, in that he tried to experience the legend directly, as opposed to merely speaking about it in the abstract. The miners' choice to quit was also an ostensive act, perhaps even a more dramatic one, in that they chose to quit their jobs because of the legend itself.

A final Tommyknocker legend from Bancroft's fieldwork follows a similar formula. Johnny Mollard, the foreman of the Argo Tunnel in Idaho Springs, detailed how one Cousin Jack quit his job because "Tommyknockers and whistle-cats [were] in there all the time."[155] Once again, this miner took to ostensive action by quitting his job because of the presence of these creatures. Like the Perigo and Chain-O-Mines examples, these narratives are tied to another specific location in the Central City District: the Argo Tunnel, which still sits prominently in the hills overlooking Idaho Springs and I-70 headed west to Colorado's ski resorts.

Although Bancroft was doing her fieldwork in the 1940s, she noted that literal belief in the Tommyknockers seemed to be diminishing.[156] However, the decline in belief did not signal the end of the Tommyknockers' reign in the Central City District. In 1994, the Tommyknocker Brewery was opened in downtown Idaho Springs. The brewery draws directly on the image of the Tommyknocker and the local mining heritage to create a distinct local image. Growing up in neighboring Evergreen, I went to the Tommyknocker Brewery often, and it was through the business that I received knowledge of these beings, rather than the "traditional" model of word-of-mouth transmission of folk culture. The brewery, which sits directly underneath the Argo Mine, had a palpable effect on my imagination. I, like the miners before me, "populated" the mountains, imagining the Tommyknockers running through them. As an elementary schooler, my class took a field trip to the Argo Mine, and because of my knowledge of the beings as I received them from the brewery, I imagine that they were in the deep caverns that we were exploring.

The Tommyknocker Brewery uses the image of the Tommyknocker to create their own brand, but in doing so they also create a regional and local identity tied to the creature. Matthew Patton and Adam Matthews, in their exploration of the connection between craft breweries and local identity, show how the Tommyknocker Brewery has used a thematic beer map to connect their brewery to both surrounding ski areas, Tommyknocker lore and local mining history.[157] They argue that Tommyknocker Brewery is an instance of "neolocalism," which is "a deliberate seeking out of regional lore and local attachment by residents (new and old) as a delayed reaction to the destruction in America of traditional bonds to community and family."[158] In other words, Tommyknocker Brewery is used as a way to connect local heritage and folklore to contemporary culture. In doing so, Colorado's regional identity is both defined and expressed through the image of the Tommyknocker.

The monster always escapes, Jeffrey Jerome Cohen proclaims in his defining essay on monster theory. The monster's power, Cohen says, comes from its "propensity to shift."[159] I might turn this notion on its head,

The Tommyknocker Brewery in Idaho Springs. *Photo by author.*

saying that while the monster always escapes, it also always returns. The knocker escaped Cornwall and shifted to fit new American and Coloradan contexts, becoming the Tommyknocker. No longer was it a Jewish ghost but the ghosts of dead miners. And while belief may have been gradually disappearing, they were still involved in the pursuit of profit, becoming the figurehead of a lucrative (and now international) craft brewery. The underground beings became aboveground symbols of regional identity and American innovation.

Tommyknockers in *Ghost Adventures* "Colorado Gold Mine" (2016)

Was Bancroft correct in her evaluation of the Tommyknockers as being part of a dying belief system in the early 1900s? The answer, as is typical in folklore, is not so cut-and-dry. The popular television program *Ghost Adventures* visited Idaho Springs in its 2016 episode "Colorado Gold Mine." *Ghost Adventures* is a television show that has aired since 2008, in which the host Zak Bagans and a group of paranormal researchers visit sites associated with ghosts and the supernatural in hopes of catching evidence of their existence. During each episode, they spend the night in a purportedly haunted location and use equipment in an attempt to elicit responses from the supernatural. In the "Colorado Gold Mine" episode, folklore of the Tommyknocker and vernacular belief in the being figured heavily into their explorations.

The journeys that paranormal researchers go on in their television shows mirror what folklorists refer to as a "legend trip." Since the 1970s, the term *legend trip* has been used to describe the act of traveling to a location associated with a legend, which often consists of performing ritual initiatory

Idaho Springs. *Wikimedia Commons.*

acts in hopes of interacting with the supernatural. Bill Ellis's article "Legend Tripping in Ohio: A Behavioral Survey" argues that legend trips are often "rituals acts of rebellion" that are done by teenagers during a liminal life stage to negotiate their relationship with societal norms.[160] Legend trips are not only undertaken by teenagers, however, and they are not always done to "give the finger" to adults, as Ellis described it. Adults often go on legend trips, and their motives are as multifaceted as the trips themselves. Legend trips are a specific iteration of ostension, as they are physical enactments of a legend through interacting with them.

Mikel Koven's work on what he calls the "convergence" of folklore and how it is portrayed in popular media is illuminating for my analysis. He notes that episodes of *Most Haunted* follow the structure of a legend trip.[161] Bill Ellis defines the structure of a legend trip as constituting "accounts of past happenings, journey into uncanny territory, contact with the supernatural, and conclude with an intense discussion."[162] Similarly, Kenneth Thigpen defined a tripartite structure in journeys to haunted locations: storytelling, ritual enactment and discussion.[163] During the "Colorado Gold Mine" episode, Zak and his crew travel to Idaho Springs, discussing local legends of ghosts and Tommyknockers haunting the mines. They then use modern ghost hunting equipment and techniques to try to elicit responses from these supernatural beings and conclude the episode with a discussion of their findings.

It is important to clarify how I define a legend, as the emic folklorist's definition of the term can at times differ from how it is used in common parlance, where it is often used interchangeably with similar but different terms such as *myth*, *folktale* or *fable*. As Linda Kinsey Adams defines them, legends are "stories people tell about events that purportedly really happened."[164] They are narratives that are set in a historical place and a historic time that are plausible or possible, and they often have a supernatural element to them. The Tommyknocker, especially as it appears in *Ghost Adventures*, falls directly into this definition.

The episode begins with Zak and his crew driving through Idaho Springs, Colorado. They are headed to the Phoenix Gold Mine, which they say is "full of ghosts." Bill Ellis notes that the automobile is a key aspect of a legend trip, in that it provides a way for accessing remote sites and as a venue for relating the legends they are about to encounter.[165] When the crew arrives at the gold

Phoenix Gold Mine in Idaho Springs. *Photo by Shari Garland on Wikimedia Commons.*

mine, they speak with tour guides at the site, who say that there are ashes that have been spread in the site, particularly those of an ex-tour guide named "Uncle Ray," who allegedly practiced black magic. In their book *Haunting Experiences: Ghosts in Contemporary Folklore*, Diane Goldstein, Sylvia Ann Grider and Jeannie Banks Thomas argue that ghost tours are one of the primary ways that the supernatural is encountered in the modern world.[166] Although tours at the Phoenix Gold Mine are not explicitly ghost tours, stories about ghosts and Tommyknockers figure in the tours.

After an initial investigation into the nearby Comstock Mine, Zak's investigation turns to Tommyknockers. It is no surprise, of course, that the episode is in Idaho Springs, the same town as the Tommyknocker Brewery, and in the same area that Caroline Bancroft did her fieldwork some seventy years prior. In keeping with traditional definitions of Tommyknockers, the show defines these beings as "gnome-like malicious spirits that have been known to cause harm to miners."[167] The scene shifts to an interview that Zak conducted with Big Jim, one of the tour guides at the Phoenix Mine.

> *ZB: One serious question, Big Jim. Do you firmly believe that these little Tommyknocker trolls are in this mine?*
> *BJ: Yes.*
> *ZB: That's all I need to know.*
> *BJ: A mischievous one will want to drop a 10-ton boulder on your head.*
> *ZB: Do you believe it?*
> *BJ: I believe it.*
> *ZB: Do the bad ones chip away at the supports, wanting to kill the miners?*
> *BJ: I have smelled them cooking bacon in the mine before. I've smelled bacon cooking in the mountain before. More than one time.*[168]

The question of belief is at the core of Zak's discussion. Despite Bancroft and Hand's assertions that belief in the Tommyknocker was disappearing, here we have Big Jim professing his belief. But doing fieldwork and analysis of popular media such as this has problems. Koven uses the term *mass-mediated ostension* to describe how legends are presented and often dramatized through documentary forms like *Ghost Adventures*. Because of the distance between the viewer (and in my case, the researcher) and the television program, there is an inherent layer of ambiguity. The ambiguity present in the presentation of legends on *Ghost Adventures* actually plays into the genre of legends, as Koven notes "the legend trip (as ostension) recognizes the ambivalence of the legend genre itself, which encourages neither belief nor disbelief, as essentialist categories, but rather a metatextual debate about whether such events are possible."[169] This distance between the viewer and the show adds a layer of debate to the already ambiguous legend being investigated.

As the episode continues, Zak and the crew do their night investigation of the mine itself, where the Tommyknockers, the ghost of the black magician Uncle Ray and the ghosts said to inhabit the mine are intertwined. They use modern ghost hunting equipment such as spirit boxes, thermal imaging cameras and SLS cameras, which they say will allow them to "peek inside another dimension where the mythological Tommyknockers may be hiding."[170] During their investigation, they use folk speech to try to interact with the Tommyknockers, saying, "Tommyknocker, Tommyknocker, we're here to take your gold! Let us hear your knock!"[171]—an interesting inversion of the knockers' warnings to Tom Trevorrow in Cornwall.

During the investigation portion, Zak attempts to contact the Tommyknockers. After he asks if they can hear him, a knock echoes on his recording. He asks, "Is that a Tommyknocker?" and then, drawing on beliefs like those documented by Bancroft, asks, "Are you a miner?...If you died in this mine, let me know."[172] The investigation takes a turn, however, because he then asks, "if you are the spirit of Ray, if you're the warlock," and is interrupted by metallic knocks in the mine. At this point, *Ghost Adventures* is moving from the belief of Tommyknockers as being spirits of dead miners, as was documented by Bancroft, to positing that Tommyknockers can be the spirits of dead people who dabbled in the occult. After this knock, it becomes ambiguous whether they are attempting to communicate with Ray or a Tommyknocker or if they are operating on the assumption that Ray has become a Tommyknocker. Zak asks, "Ray, are you doing black magic on us?"[173] Using the SLS camera, which is used to capture anomalous forms on video, they attempt to get Ray to appear, prompting him to "show yourself."[174] Then, a figure manifests on the SLS camera, standing on top of Zak's recorder, which he interprets as Ray as a Tommyknocker.

As their investigation ends, they discuss their evidence and reflect on the experience. Zak ends the episode saying. "Between the legends of the Tommyknockers, and the very real miners who lost their lives in these dark caverns, I will never enter another mine without a deep respect for what is forever left behind in these shadows."[175] Jeannie Banks Thomas argues that ghost stories (or legends of the Tommyknockers that blur categorical boundaries) can expand our knowledge of the landscapes that surround us, while also transforming individuals' lives.[176] While there is the layer of ambiguity in this mass-mediated ostension, Zak's conclusions reflect that observation.

CONCLUSION

The knocker made the journey from Cornwall to Colorado and in the process became the Tommyknocker. In their original context, knockers were thought to be elf-like beings who were the spirits of Jewish miners. In Colorado, Tommyknockers came to be thought of as morally ambiguous spirits who were the ghosts of specific miners who worked in the mines, such as the spirit of John Q.A. Rollins in the Perigo mine. Tommyknockers became associated with hyperlocal, hyperspecific mines, particularly those located in the Central City District of Colorado, which was home to some of the state's gold rush–era centers. These beings became tied to the local industry through the creation of the Tommyknocker Brewery, which sits in downtown Idaho Springs, directly below mines associated with their legends. The tourist industry draws on the popularity of Tommyknockers to attract visitors to their sites. Finally, the television show *Ghost Adventures* presented one of the more contemporary examples of Tommyknocker explorations, mixing the legends of these beings with not only dead miners but also occult practitioners rumored to have spread their ashes in the mines. These legends, as they migrated across the Atlantic Ocean and the country, found a natural home in the mountains of Colorado and morphed to fit the natural landscape and cultural environment.

The author at a Tommyknocker-themed haunted house attraction. *Photo by author.*

5

FANTASTIC BEASTS OF COLORADO AND WHERE TO FIND THEM

A COLORADO BESTIARY

Whoever fights monsters should see to it that in the process he does not become a monster.
—Friedrich Nietzsche

Colorado is home to a number of legendary monsters. This chapter, in a sense, draws on the ancient tradition of bestiaries, which enumerate the animals said to inhabit the natural world. These bestiaries, which became extremely popular during the Middle Ages, juxtaposed "known" animals such as the frog or hamster alongside legendary creatures such as the unicorn, basilisk and harpy. A key aspect of medieval bestiaries is that they served an allegorical function. Thus, the animals themselves were thought to communicate some sort of truth, usually a Christian one. For example, the song of the sirens was thought to warn of being charmed by flattery or ostentation.[177]

The monsters of Colorado serve a similar function. The word *monster* comes from the Latin *monstrum*, meaning "that which reveals," or "that which warns."[178] Monster legends can be looked at as a metaphorical language to talk about something else. As I have done throughout the rest of the book, however, I will not discount the notion that such legends can and are rooted in personal experience: people report seeing dogmen and other strange creatures in Colorado. At the same time, I think we can look at legends of the Slide-Rock Bolter or the Augerino as commentaries on the history of labor and agriculture in the state.

In keeping with the rest of the book, this chapter focuses on the legendary creatures of Colorado. We are dealing here with what are often described as "cryptids," that is, animals whose existence is not as yet accepted by mainstream science. Cryptids are the object of discovery for the field of cryptozoology, which was defined in the twentieth century by its founder, Bernard Heuvelmans, as "the scientific study of hidden animals, i.e. of still unknown animal forms about which only testimonial and circumstantial evidence is available, or material evidence considered insufficient by some."[179] In Colorado, there are stories of out-of-place animals such as kangaroos, grizzly bears, melanistic cougars and even dinosaurs. I have chosen, however, to focus on creatures that could also be considered monsters. This is in keeping with the spirit of Heuvelmans's definitions of cryptids, where elsewhere he said that cryptids need one aspect that is "truly singular, unexpected, paradoxical, striking, emotionally upsetting, and thus capable of mythification."[180] This is certainly the case for well-known cryptids such as dogman, but this chapter also includes what are called "fearsome critters," which populated the bestiaries of early twentieth-century lumberjack tall tales. While the lines between cryptid, monster and fearsome critter are blurred and at best muddy, that is the essence of the monster, which in itself confuses boundaries and tidy orders of classification. So without further ado, let's explore the monster legends of Colorado.

AUGERINO

The Augerino is depicted as a corkscrew-shaped worm creature that is known for drilling helical holes in irrigation ditches. These malevolent worms line their underground burrows with silica to prevent cave-ins, are thought to move very slowly, are immune to all poisons and weapons and have a sole mission of messing with farmers by letting the water out of their ditches.[181] The reason for this behavior is that Augerinos are thought to inhabit Colorado's dry lands, and because of their native habitat, they try to destroy any invasive water systems.[182]

Augerinos clearly fall into the category of "fearsome critters," which are features of tall tales told by lumberjacks as pranks to scare new crew members. The authority on the Augerino is the folklorist Ronald Ives, who wrote about the creature in his 1941 article "Folklore of Middle Park, Colorado." Unfortunately, Ives described legends about the Augerino as being the result of alcohol consumption and sheer irrationality, saying, "Hallucinations reported to accompany delirium tremens might lead to the creation of such chimerical fauna."[183] Such an approach, I think, misses the point of legends as a whole.

As I have stated at many points throughout the book, and feel compelled to do so again here, my interest as a folklorist is not in debunking or proving the veracity of these legends. Rather, I operate under the assumption that legends tell us about our hopes and fears. They give us insight into what is most important to a culture. There is a reason that the Augerino appeared as a legend in the place and time that it did, so what might that reason be?

If we take a step back and observe the Augerino, we can see that it is about one specific topic: *irrigation*. This might seem like an odd topic for a legend, but irrigation, the practice of supplying water for agricultural crops, has played a crucial role in the historical development of industry in Colorado. One thing of note in this chapter, specifically in regards to the fearsome critter tall tales, is that these stories focus on the transformation of Colorado's landscape throughout the nineteenth and twentieth centuries. The Augerino, named for the auger, a drilling tool to make holes in the ground, serves as a way of looking into the history of agriculture in Colorado.

While the Centennial State is Colorado's official nickname, it has also been called the Headwaters State, owing to the importance of its many river basins. Originally, mining was the main industry that drew people to the state, but afterward agriculture replaced it, with irrigation at its core. This expansion and diversion of water meant that dry areas, such as those that the Augerino might inhabit, were now able to be used for agricultural purposes. Throughout the 1850s and into the 1870s, irrigation spread throughout the state to more distant areas. Like the legends that spread to Colorado from distant lands, so did the agricultural practices, as the Coloradan farmers used an acequia system developed by the Spanish, who learned it from the Moors. The practice of irrigation was so important to Colorado's history that Justice Greg Hobbs said, "Ditches help to invent and reinvent Colorado."[184]

Legends tend to occur and morph during times of cultural stress and change. This dramatic change in the environment evidently led tellers of tall tales, presumably lumberjacks, to invent a humorous reason for failures in irrigation in the form of the Augerino. Like the land itself, the Augerino, which prefers arid environments, had to adapt to their changing landscape. They did not simply invent the character out of thin air, however. The

Augerino resembles many sand worms from world folklore and mythology, such as the Mongolian death worm, which is said to be full of deathly poison; the Indus worm, which dates back to the fifth century CE and was full of valuable oil; and the Icelandic Lagarfljot worm, which, like the Augerino, is said to bring about crop failure. Even the Augerino's immunity to poison and weapons is reminiscent of European dragons.

Ives does provide one interesting explanation for the Augerino, saying that their descriptions may be the misinterpretation of paleontological evidence, citing their similarity in appearance to "Devil's Corkscrews," which are the internal molds of the Cretaceous gastropod Laxispira, which are sometimes called fossil Augerinos.[185] Ives's suspicions seemed to be in a sense prophetic, as in 2008 a helical fossil discovered in New Mexico was named *Augerinoichnus helicoidalis* after the legendary Augerino. Such instances are known as "geomythology"—that is, the influence of mythology and folklore in the realm of geology.

DOGMAN

The image of a human-canine hybrid comes to us from classical antiquity and ancient mythology. Ovid's *Metamorphoses* (8 CE) tells of how King Lycaon was transformed into a wolfman by Jupiter after failing to recognize the god and subsequently attempting to feed him human flesh. This resulted in Lycaon's transformation for his exterior to mirror his inner beast. Ram Dass might qualify this early myth as having the moralistic coda of treating everyone as god in drag. The Egyptian god Anubis was depicted as being jackal-headed and presided over the role of psychopomp in the underworld/afterlife known as the Duat. Cyanocephali, or dog-headed humans, have a role in Catholic hagiography and theology, as St. Augustine wrote about them in his *City of God* (fifth century AD) and St. Christopher is occasionally depicted with the head of a dog. The werewolf is a crucial figure in European occult history, including the infamous cases of Peter Stubbe and his magic belt, Jean Grenier and his potent salve, the murderous rampage of the Beast of Gevaudan and citations in critical texts such as James I's *Demonology*, Reginald Scot's *Discoverie of Witchcraft* and the infamous *Malleus Maleficarum*.

Recently, however, the trend in the United States is to identify human-canine hybrids as "dogman." These legends extend to the 1980s in Michigan with stories about the Michigan Dogman, which intensified with the work of the reporter Linda Godfrey and her reports about a creature called the Beast of Bray Road in Elkhorn, Wisconsin. Godfrey noticed that a local policeman had a file titled "werewolf" and began to document extensive sightings of a strange werewolf-like creature in the area. Nowadays, the terms *werewolf* and *dogman* seem to be used interchangeably.

Unsurprisingly, this ancient migratory legend has found an expression in Colorado. For the most part, stories about dogman in Colorado come in the form of memorates, the narrative form cited extensively throughout this book, but to reiterate are personal narratives about the supernatural. The online archive North American Dogman Project (NADP), whose mission is similar to the Bigfoot Field Researchers Organization (BFRO) from the bigfoot chapter, includes two memorates from Colorado. The first comes from Prowers County in southeastern Colorado:

> *I was getting home late one day.…That's when I saw this thing. At first, I thought it was a coyote. A BIG coyote! It was almost 5 feet tall, on all fours! It was caught in my trap and was running around, making a dust cloud, and then it stopped and looked at me.…I was looking at it in shock*

King Lycaon and Jupiter. *Wikimedia Commons.*

> *and awe and noticed that it had orange eyes....It then growled at me and then it was gone in the blink of an eye.*[186]

This memorate, as many of them do, includes rhetorical strategies to enhance the strength of the narrator. This includes the alternative explanation (a coyote), a detailed description (cat eyes, hands, not paws) and an emotional connection of how terrifying the encounter was.

A second memorate from the NADP database comes from Pueblo:

> *The dogman has been sighted off Lime Road which also borders my river....My researchers had me put out cams to see if I could catch any Bigfoot activity. I did, and over the years have caught other strange creatures on cam. I call them hybrids....I have a pic of the dogman I caught in the river....He has huge shoulders and is staring directly at the camera across from it. Yes, it is black, has ears that tip in towards themselves, and scars on its face....Gentlemen, be very careful with going into the woods with these things. I can prove these creatures, and the others are not what we know as normal animals. Dogmen are very hard to kill as well as Bigfoot or as well as the other creatures on my place....Dogman, Bigfoot and the other crypts out there are giants of old.*[187]

Often, as is the case here, paranormal phenomena are seen as being interrelated and tied to more ancient traditions, such as the "giants of old," presumably the biblical Nephilim. Narratives such as this allow researchers to dissect the peculiarities of belief, specifically how "dogman" is used instead of "werewolf"; how the legend is considered in connection to other supernatural phenomena such as Bigfoot; and how they are connected to ancient tradition. For the sake of this chapter, these two narratives suffice to demonstrate that werewolf/dogman legends have found expression in Colorado, but I was able to identify several other Colorado dogman memorates in podcasts and secondary sources.

THE GOG MONSTER

While I dedicate an entire chapter of this book to Bigfoot, what I did not mention is that in the United States there are many hyperlocal variants of the cryptid. These variants include the Ohio Grassman, West Virginia's

Grafton Monster, North Carolina's Tsul 'Kalu and Pennsylvania's Albatwitch. In Colorado, our variant is called the GOG Monster. This creature is said to be a Bigfoot-like being, standing seven to eight feet tall with reddish brown hair. It gets its name from Colorado Springs' Garden

Balanced rock, Garden of the Gods. *Library of Congress.*

Cathedral Spires, Garden of the Gods. *Library of Congress.*

of the Gods, where it is rumored to haunt hidden passages and secret tunnels.[188]

Legends about the GOG Monster were evidently known to locals by the mid-1960s, when an individual named Doc Smokey and his friends were riding bicycles around the park at night. Doc shared the following memorate of his encounter with the creature:

> *My friend Dave said he thought he saw something moving in the moonlight about two hundred feet down the roadway. We saw nothing, so we relaxed. About five minutes later, Dave said, "Look!" and pointed down the road again. This time, we all saw this big, shaggy bulk slowly heading in our direction. He was about a hundred feet away, but we could distinctly see the glowing reddish yellow eyes.*[189]

Dave's memorate is consistent with the adolescent legend trip mentioned earlier in the book. He and his friends traveled to the site associated with the supernatural and encountered a personal interaction with the uncanny.

As we have seen earlier in our discussion of lake monsters, mysterious tunnels breed legends. Not only is the Garden of the Gods full of hazardous tunnels, many of which have been closed down, and are in themselves dangerous and therefore a perfect location for stories of the supernatural, but Colorado Springs is also home to one of the nation's foremost subterranean lairs: NORAD. This aerospace command center has a facility located inside of Colorado Springs' Cheyenne Mountain. It is curious that legends about secret tunnels at the nearby Garden of the Gods have inspired stories about strange creatures. Perhaps Colorado Springs' many underground labyrinths are interconnected in their legend complexes.

THE HATCHET LADY OF RED ROCKS

Monsters disrupt and complicate our tidy and organized orders of classification. One urban legend from Colorado that exemplifies this is the Hatchet Lady of Red Rocks, a character who is not "monstrous" in the sense that the dogman is as a dog-human hybrid but nonetheless warrants a discussion in this chapter for the reason that, well, she doesn't belong anywhere else in this book. The Hatchet Lady legend tells of a figure stalking the roads along Red Rocks Amphitheatre waiting to chop the arm off of adolescents. The legend scholar par excellence Bill Ellis has stressed the importance of providing verbatim versions of legends,[190] and the Hatchet Lady legend as it was documented by the folklorist Linda Dégh goes like this:

> *A group of people (four girls and four guys) went to Red Rocks for a drive. Just to have a good time and be together as friends. The scene was, two couples in the back seat and two in the front. It was supposed to be a joke and ended up seriously. The joke was: have a girl (not from the group) dress up as a ghost (like the little girl), come up to the parked car and scare the couples. But not the real girl came up to the car. The two couples in the back seat were mortified. The guy on the driver's side had had his arm outside the window and the Hatchet Lady cut it off. The two couples who were in the back seat are now in the mental hospital.*[191]

The Hatchet Lady of Red Rocks is a local variant of an urban legend that folklorists call "The Hook." This urban legend is so widespread and well-known that an image of a hook hanging from a car has become almost

Red Rocks Amphitheater. *Photo by Scalper on Wikimedia Commons.*

synonymous with urban legends. Often, urban legends, or what some folklorists call contemporary legends, focus on the period of adolescence right before adulthood and stress the transitory rites of sexuality, the exploration of social norms and the use of new technologies such as the car and therefore new freedoms.

In the Hatchet Lady legend, these individuals are clearly meant to be engaging, or potentially engaging, in sexual activity. One theory to explain the hook legend is Alan Dundes's Freudian reading that the cut off hand is symbolically equivalent to the phallus and therefore is a symbolic castration.[192] In that reading, the Hatchet Lady of Red Rocks serves as a warning against adolescent sexuality. Other possible fears and anxieties this legend articulates are fears about driving and parking in general, parents' concerns for their children and antisocial people.[193]

The physical location of the legend is also very revealing. Red Rocks Amphitheatre is not only one of Colorado's most famous places but also the axis mundi for bacchanalian revelry in the state. Alcohol and mind-altering substance consumption are rampant at the venue. I recall urban legends that circulated at my high school about adolescents taking too much LSD at the venue and being found by the police crawling on the side of the road. The Hatchet Lady legend, in part, warns about the potential results from overindulging at the famous venue's concerts.

SLIDE-ROCK BOLTER

If you were to ask someone familiar with Colorado folklore what the state's most famous cryptid is, chances are they'd say the Slide-Rock Bolter. This creature is depicted as a giant land whale that latches itself to the sides of mountains that have slopes greater than forty-five degrees. It sits, waiting for tourists to pass through the valley below, at which point it will detach itself and devour the visitor to its terrain. Stories about the Slide-Rock Bolter were popularized by William Thomas Cox's 1910 *Fearsome Critters of the Lumberwoods*. Cox, who was Minnesota's first state forester, wrote the book in order to document tall tales of lumberjacks. The full text given on the Slide-Rock Bolter is as follows:

> *In the mountains of Colorado, where in summer the woods are becoming infested with tourists, much uneasiness has been caused by the presence of the slide-rock bolter. This frightful animal lives only in the steepest mountain country where the slopes are greater than 45 degrees. It has an immense head, with small eyes, and a mouth somewhat on the order of a sculpin, running back beyond its ears. The tail consists of a divided flipper, with enormous grab-hooks, which it fastens over the crest of the mountain or ridge, often remaining there motionless for days at a time, watching the gulch for tourists or any other hapless creature that may enter it. At the right moment, after sighting a tourist, it will lift its tail, thus loosening its hold on the mountain, and with its small eyes riveted on the poor unfortunate, and drooling thin skid grease from the corners of its mouth, which greatly accelerates its speed, the bolter comes down like a toboggan, scooping in its victim as it goes, its own impetus carrying it up the next slope, where it again slaps its tail over the ridge and waits. Whole parties of tourists are reported to have been gulped at one swoop by the slide-rock bolter, and guides are becoming cautious about taking parties far back into the hills. The animal is a menace not only to tourists but to the woods as well. Many a draw through spruce-covered slopes has been laid low, the trees being*

Top: Ophir Loop on the Rio Grande Southern Railroad, 1892. *Library of Congress.*

Bottom: Ophir Loop, Colorado, United States, 1909. *Library of Congress.*

Opposite: Sheep Mountain from Lizard Head Pass. *Photo by user sf-dvs on Wikimedia Commons.*

knocked out by the roots or mowed off as by a scythe where the bolter has crashed down through from the peaks above.

A forest ranger, whose district includes the rough country between Ophir Peaks and the Lizzard Head, conceived the bold idea of decoying a slide-rock bolter to its own destruction. A dummy tourist was rigged up with plaid Norfolk jacket, knee breeches, and a guide book to Colorado. It was then filled full of giant powder and fulminate caps and posted in a

conspicuous place, where, sure enough, the next day it attracted the attention of a bolter which had been hanging for days on the slope of Lizzard Head. The resulting explosion flattened half the buildings in Rico, which were never rebuilt, and the surrounding hills fattened flocks of buzzards the rest of the summer.[194]

When looking at this entry about the Slide-Rock Bolter, several idiosyncratic details emerge. First, there is the very specific geographical location that is mentioned: the area between Ophir Peaks and Lizzard Head (today spelled Lizard Head). This puts the story of the Slide-Rock Bolter in southwestern Colorado near the old mining town Rico. Second, there is a focus on the tourist wearing a Norfolk jacket, which was a popular fashion among East Coasters during the time period. What are we to do with these details? It seems that the Slide-Rock Bolter is trying to tell us something about the state of the lumberjack industry near the Ophir Peaks and Lizard Head during the early 1900s.[195]

The town of Rico experienced a boom during the gold rush. The area, which had been Ute territory due to the treaty of 1868, was open for mining by Americans following the Brunot Agreement. By 1892, Rico had experienced a surge in mining industries, and many businesses moved in to capitalize on the success. But in 1893, the town experienced a silver panic, causing a mass exodus. After the mining industry left, the lumber industry moved in and began a campaign of deforestation to both support statewide mining as well as the need for railroad timber. As you drive through the highways of Colorado, you often see gashes of rubble on the sides of mountains. These are often the marks of abandoned mines. The lumberjacks of Rico likely saw these and used the Slide-Rock Bolter as a tongue-in-cheek explanation for their presence. The explosion caused by the tourist trap would explain their

Top: Rico, Colorado. *Library of Congress.*

Bottom: Rico Courthouse. *Photo by Eric S. Kounce, Wikimedia Commons CC BY 3.0.*

dilapidated houses, but it also explains why a tourist would be necessary for the story in the first place. Due to the deforestation, conservationists and eco-tourists fought for environmental protections in Colorado. The lumberjacks would have seen them as responsible for their industry's decline, ironically not seeing the harmful effects they were causing.[196]

THE TROLL OF BRECKENRIDGE

What, you might ask, is the connection between Colorado and the Norse god Odin, the one-eyed all-father who sacrificed himself to himself on the World Tree for magical knowledge? Or perhaps you may be curious about the connection between Thor the Thunderer, slayer of giants and trolls, and the mountains of Colorado. Maybe these are only questions I think about. Yet there are connections, and they can be found nestled in the forests of Breckenridge and near the mountains of Cripple Creek. I am talking, of course, about Isak Heartstone and Rita the Rock Planter, which are giant wooden troll sculptures made by the Danish artist Thomas Dambo. While these are not legends, like the other beasts of these chapters, they deserve recognition not only because of their popularity but also the ways they tie Colorado's culture to a broader mythology.

Dambo's one hundred troll sculptures can be found in seventeen different countries. We are lucky enough to have two of them in Colorado. Isak Heartstone, the Troll of Breckenridge, can be found by taking a short walk through Trollstigen Trail in Breckenridge. Dambo's second Colorado sculpture, Rita the Rock Planter, is located near a nineteenth-century gold mine in Cripple Creek. Rita is depicted patching up holes in the earth from the mine as a representation of the environmental efforts necessary to repair human-generated damage. Dambo makes a poem for each of his trolls, and Rita's is this:

> *A hundred suns is how long a nap takes for the trolls*
> *When Rita woke again, her mountainside was full of holes*
> *The humans must have dug them in their search for shiny rock*
> *But someone could fall in, so Rita went to tidy up.*[197]

The Trolls of Breckenridge and Cripple Creek serve as environmental metaphors, but they also enchant the landscape and the lives of their

This page and opposite: The Troll of Breckenridge created by Danish artist Thomas Dambo. *Photo by Anthony Quintano, Flikr CC BY 2.0.*

visitors. Trolls in mythology and folklore serve a similar function, as the verb *trolla/trylla* means "to enchant" or "to carry out magic."[198] Like Rita the Rock Planter, mythological trolls not only modified the landscape but occasionally helped form it during primordial time as well.[199] Trolls, which is often an all-purpose word for supernatural beings such as giants, appear frequently in Norse epics, including the Poetic Edda, where Thor battles them frequently. Our local trolls in Colorado remind us to be ecologically minded and aware of our connection to the natural environment.

THE VAMPIRE OF LAFAYETTE

One of the strangest legends in Colorado centers on a gravestone in Lafayette that, rumors say, is the grave of a vampire. The grave, which sits in Lafayette's municipal cemetery, marks the resting spot of Fodor Glava, who was born in Transylvania before immigrating to America. By all accounts, Glava likely worked as a miner before dying in 1918 at the height of the Spanish flu epidemic.[200] Legends about the grave say that locals, suspecting Glava as a vampire, dug up his grave only to find him with fresh

Vampire grave. *Photo by author.*

blood on his mouth and his nails still growing. They drove a stake through his heart, and the legends hold it grew into a tree that can still be seen there today.[201] Paranormal researchers have reported an assemblage of spooky phenomena at the grave, including shadow figures, battery drainage and disembodied voices.[202]

By 1918, Transylvania and the figure of the vampire were intimately linked in the public consciousness through the publication and popularity of Bram Stoker's *Dracula* (1897). The literary character of Dracula was inspired in part by the historical figure Vlad Tepes, a fifteenth-century Romanian count who has an ambiguous legacy as the first ruler to unify Wallachia, Romania and Transylvania, but he did so by dubious means such as burning political opponents alive, poisoning wells and impaling opposing army combatants, a practice that earned him the sobriquet "Vlad the Impaler."

The vampire of folklore, however, was in many ways quite different from the suave Romanian count of Stoker's. The folkloric vampire was not typically handsome and aristocratic but rather disheveled, poorly dressed, plump and bearded. The first usage of a term etymologically linked to *vampire* comes from Russia in 1047, when the word *upir* was used.[203] A upir is a type of revenant, which is a reanimated corpse come back to haunt the world of the living. Vampires, then, are traditionally a sort of revenant, but in Europe they were related to an assemblage of other creatures such as the Romanian strigoi, the Greek vrykolakas and the Albanian shtriga.[204]

What is most notable about the vampire of Lafayette is that he is said to have died during the Spanish flu epidemic of 1918. Historically, vampires and epidemics have been closely linked. One way of identifying a vampire postmortem is if many of their family or villagers die soon after.[205] The story of Fodor Glava mirrors the case of Peter Plogojowitz, a German man who died in 1725. Shortly after his death, nine other people died. Villagers exhumed Peter's body and found that his body was undecomposed, with his hair and nails still growing. The townsfolk then pierced his heart with a wooden stake.[206] These are all signs of rigor mortis, or how the body decays after death. Blood coming from the mouth, bloating, growing hair or nails—these are all attributes of supposed vampires but are just mistaken natural processes. Even sounds coming from the grave are the releases of gasses from the body. The case of Fodor Glava, then, is an example of how xenophobia of Transylvanians, paranoia during a time of epidemic and misattributions with natural decay with vampirism resulted in his identification as a vampire.

WEBFOOTED HORSES

The Great Sand Dunes in southern Colorado are said to be home to a most mysterious creature: webfooted horses. These horses are said to have developed webbed feet in order to allow them to move across the difficult, sandy terrain. It is believed that they appear on full moon nights and are much larger than typical horses. Nestled within the San Luis Valley, the Great Sand Dunes are home to other mysterious phenomena as well, including singing sands, voices coming from the great beyond, a mysterious hum and UFO sightings.[207]

While Colorado's webfooted horses have found a unique ecological niche in the sand dunes, we can think of these legends as being a local expression of a much larger tradition: water horses from folklore. The most famous of these water horses is the kelpie, a shape-shifter from Scottish and Irish folklore that also has webbed feet. Unlike the webfooted horses of Colorado and their sandy terrain, however, the kelpie aims to tempt travelers to get on its back, at which point the victim realizes they

The Great Sand Dunes. *Library of Congress.*

cannot escape. The creature will then take them to its underground lair and devour them. Kelpies do have one weak point though: if the rider can grab hold of its bridle, they can take control of the aquatic monster. Other famous water horses from folklore include the cabbyl-ushtey from Celtic folklore, which also emerges from waters to abduct and devour, and the aughisky, which is said to eat cattle but will also gallop over sands during the winter.[208]

While the webfooted horses of the Great Sand Dunes seem to be a regional variant of these Celtic creatures, we must ask ourselves why such legends appear in this specific area of Colorado. Both a postcolonial critique and a critical environmental theory approach can be applied here. Horses and the Great Sand Dunes are intertwined with the complicated history of the location. Beginning in the sixteenth century, Spanish explorers entered the San Luis Valley, where Indigenous people had lived for thousands of years, and in 1776, Juan Bautista de Anza led a raid against the local Comanche on horseback. These legends can be seen, I think, as a commentary on the complicated colonial legacy of the region.

Then again, stories about webfooted horses at the Great Sand Dunes also speak of the agency of the land and the terrain itself, hinting at the harsh and difficult climate that necessitate the growth of new feet to pass through the singing sands.

CONCLUSION

Throughout the book, we've seen how folklore is hidden in plain sight. While most of us go about our days without a thought to the supernatural, the creatures from this bestiary lurk in the liminal zones between our fears and anxieties. Dogman and the GOG monster are creatures who exist in the memorates of people who purport to have seen them. The Augerino and Slide-Rock Bolter come from tall tales of lumberjacks but tell us crucial information about the development of industry and technology in the state. The Hatchet Lady of Red Rocks is a local version of a famous urban legend, "The Hook," which warns about the dangers of adult sexuality and overconsumption of substances. The Trolls of Breckenridge and Cripple Creek, alongside the Vampire of Lafayette and the Great Sand Dunes' webfooted horses, show the long migratory journey that Europe's monsters made to find an ecological niche in Colorado. These monsters serve as mirrors to our culture and, through our examination, allow us to learn crucial details about ourselves.

PART II

INCORPOREAL LEGENDS

6
THE COLORADO HORROR

HAUNTED HOUSES

Nothing, not bonds of steel or prayer, can restrain the Dionysian forces that lurk just beneath the placid surface of everyday life.
—David Bailey

The house," Henry Glassie says, "is the logical center for American history."[209] The American landscape is covered in houses of every different style and shape. Their form, material and style materialize historical time and thought. But the American landscape, and by extension the Colorado landscape, is also covered with haunted houses. These haunted houses loom, both literally and metaphorically, over our collective culture. Archetypally, they often sit on top of hills and are occupied by aristocrats and the elite. On the metaphorical level, David Bailey, who developed what he called the "haunted house formula," argues that "the haunted house finally seems like nothing less than a symbol of America and the American mind, of all the ghosts that haunt us, from the dark legacy of slavery to the failed war in Vietnam."[210] The haunted house in Colorado serves as a regional representation of both an idea and as a physical location.

Growing up as a child in Kittredge, Colorado, I remember hearing stories that a house in the neighborhood was haunted. From my recollection, the story was that a man had gone crazy in the house and that his spirit lingered there. In my imagination, I had chosen one of the houses in the neighborhood as this haunted location. Haunted houses, Sylvia Ann Grider explains, "gain the reputation for being haunted simply on the basis of how closely they resemble the iconic haunted house of oral tradition and literature."[211] I had identified the haunted house simply because I knew what the archetypal haunted house looked like. While I was out trick-or-treating as a seven-year-old in that neighborhood, I swore I saw the ghost of a crazy man staring out of one of the windows of the creepy house, in alignment with the "dark, vague, ephemeral creatures and apparitions [that] drift through haunted houses."[212]

David Bailey argues that the image of the haunted house owes its origins to the Gothic novel, particularly Horace Walpole's 1764 *Castle of Otranto.*[213] The dark and gloomy settings of Gothic novels made the haunted house a lasting image in American culture. To be clear, when I speak of the haunted house, I'm speaking about houses themselves as opposed to carnival attractions. The haunted house became clearly identifiable as having "distinctive mansard roofs, towers and turrets, multiple stories, and ornate architectural embellishments," and due to their style and grandeur, they "became symbols of opulence and decadence."[214] Because of their style, mansions owned by wealthy people often became identified as being haunted, especially after their passing. In Colorado, the case is no different, as this chapter looks at mansions such as the Peabody-Whitehead Mansion, the Croke-Patterson Mansion, the Hindry House and the Molly Brown House. All of these houses meet the archetypal image of the haunted house. Perhaps since these were spaces that the polis were not able to inhabit, they populated them with tales of hauntings and the uncanny.

Bailey's *American Nightmares: The Haunted House Formula in American Popular Fiction* sees the haunted house, like Glassie sees the house itself, as a potent symbol of American culture. He says, "The haunted house finally seems like nothing less than a symbol of America and the American mind, of all the ghosts that haunt us, from the dark legacy of slavery to the failed war in Vietnam."[215] By analyzing haunted houses through the classic "myth and symbol school" of American studies—that is, identifying important cultural mores and attitudes through symbols and literature—Bailey sees this image as a place where authors can inscribe important fears, anxieties and ideas from American history. As is the case with many topics in folklore, there is a tension between experience and a metaphorical or allegorical explanation for them. At times, of course, people's understanding of a house as being haunted is because of personal experiences they have had inside the place. Much of the literature about haunted houses in Colorado takes the approach of sharing the stories of hauntings, assuming that is enough to entertain the readers. Perhaps it is, but as an academic I hope to deconstruct the cultural meanings at work in these legends while also acknowledging that for people who have experienced the terrors of a haunted house this metaphorical deconstruction may not suffice. When you look at famous haunted houses in Colorado, there is often some sort of taboo or cultural anxiety at play, which often occur along the axes of class and gender, economic hardship and consequences of the past that Bailey identified in his formula. It is no surprise that haunted houses are mansions of the ultra-rich: those excluded from that space are bound to populate them with legend and rumor.

THE CROKE-PATTERSON MANSION

One of Colorado's most famous haunted houses is the Croke-Patterson Mansion at 420 East Eleventh Avenue in Denver. The house was built in 1890 for one of the most successful businessmen in Denver, Thomas Bernard Croke, who decided to sell the property just six months after building it. The house is home to many legends, including the ghost of his wife, Kate Patterson; disembodied voices; ghost babies in the basement; spectral hounds; and a ghostly woman at the top of the stairs.[216] Many of these legends reflect larger cultural anxieties. Kate is said to appear as a pregnant woman, with

The Croke-Patterson Mansion. *Photo by Jeffrey Beall, Wikimedia Commons.*

childbirth being a liminal stage where both life and death are confronted. Adolescent deaths in the basement are especially potent in Colorado, where JonBenét Ramsey was found dead in 1996. The basement itself is a potent symbol in haunted houses, as it is associated with symbols of evil, in touch with supernatural forces because of its underground location, subliminally connected to castle dungeons and torture chambers, and is the location of real murder victims.[217] Spectral hounds are a staple of world folklore, as can be seen through the hellhounds of British folklore, the mythical Cù Sìth of Celtic mythology and Cwn Annwn of Welsh lore. The top of the stairs is often a common place for ghost legends, as the staircase itself is a liminal zone connecting one place to the next.

THE MOLLY BROWN HOUSE

Another famous haunted house in Denver is the Molly Brown House. A potent memory from my childhood was visiting this house, where I struck up a strange fascination with the historical figure of Molly Brown. This

Molly Brown House. *Courtesy of www.mollybrown.org from Wikimedia Commons CC BY 4.0.*

Victorian parlor of the Molly Brown House and Museum in Denver, Colorado. *Photo by Carol M. Highsmith, Library of Congress.*

fascination with Molly Brown seems to grip many people. Serendipitously, while at Pennsylvania State University–Harrisburg's celebration of the doctoral program's anniversary, a presenter I had never met before mentioned she worked at the Molly Brown House. She told me that while she worked there, she remembered stories of ghostly cigar smoke filling the air. The house, which sits at 1340 Pennsylvania Street, is a visually striking residence. Molly Brown was famous for, in part, being one of the few survivors of the *Titanic*. Though we remember her today as Molly, this was purely a Hollywood invention: she came to be known as that from the movie *The Unsinkable Molly Brown*—in her life she was always known as Margaret.[218] The concept of "hauntology," created by Jacques Derrida and expanded on by postmodernist philosophers such as Mark Fisher, holds that we are haunted by imagined pasts and aborted futures. A haunting "happens when a place is stained by time, or when a particular place becomes the site for an encounter with broken time."[219] The cultural Mandelian misremembering of Margaret's name lends credence to her

The Molly Brown House Museum in Denver, Colorado. *Photo by Carol M. Highsmith, Library of Congress.*

hauntological stature in Colorado's history. During her life, she and her husband, J.J., were staples in elite society and gained their riches through mining entrepreneurship, arguably the single most influential industry in the history of Colorado.

During her life, Molly had an interest in the spiritualist movement, which entailed holding séances, tarot card readings and visiting fortune tellers. Shortly before boarding *Titanic*, she visited a medium who said she saw disaster involving water in her future.[220] Some of the legends at the Molly Brown House include ghost cats, the smell of J.J.'s cigar smoke and dark figures, presumably the ghosts of Molly's nephew Frank, who died of scarlet fever at the house, or Brown's mother, Johanna.[221] The ghost cat is a common motif, identified as E521.3 in the *Motif-Index of Folk-Literature*.[222] Frank's story indicates a fear over death at a young age, particularly from a disease, and J.J. was not allowed to smoke in the house—this taboo violation hangs over the manor even in death.

The Peabody-Whitehead Mansion

Another famous haunted mansion in Denver is the Peabody-Whitehead Mansion, built in 1889 and located at Eleventh and Grant in Denver. This Victorian Queen Anne–style mansion derives its name from two of its infamous inhabitants: Dr. William Riddick Whitehead, a former surgeon for the Confederate army, and Governor James Peabody, notorious for fostering poor wages and standards of living for Colorado miners. After the home was remodeled as a restaurant in the 1960s, rumors began to circulate that the house was haunted by soldiers who died under Whitehead's care. As Bailey

The Peabody-Whitehead Mansion. *Photo by Jeffrey Beall, Wikimedia Commons.*

reminds us, the haunted house is the place where the ghosts that haunt us culturally manifest themselves.[223] What haunts America more than the Civil War? The Peabody-Whitehead Mansion reminds us of this terrible history, and although Colorado was geographically removed from the battlegrounds of the Civil War, its specters continue to haunt the state.[224]

THE HINDRY HOUSE

That is not to say these archetypal haunted houses don't carry a haunted reputation. In fact, Colorado is full of them. One of the most famous haunted houses in Colorado is the Hindry House. Although the house burned down in 1962, in its heyday this palatial estate conformed to the iconic haunted house image. A 1948 article from the *Rocky Mountain News* attests to its haunted form: "The old house is perfectly cast for its role of 'haunted.'...On moonlight nights, when lights within are extinguished, its high, narrow windows stare like vacant eyes, and old Hindry's vengeful ghost is said to walk the halls."[225] Like many haunted houses, the Hindry House gained a reputation as being haunted in part because it *looked* like a haunted house. But these places don't always gain such a reputation based on their aesthetic merit: there is often a real history that accompanies their notoriety. Such is the case of the Hindry House.

In 1858, John Hindry moved to Colorado from New York shortly after the discovery of gold in the area. A contractor by trade, Hindry saw opportunity for riches in Colorado because of the expanding economy as a result of the gold rush. He opened a sawmill in Bear Creek Canyon, which provided the lumber for many of Denver's new buildings. Hindry parlayed this success into starting a cattle ranch in what is now the town of Masters. By 1870, Hindry had amassed an impressive fortune, and he used his money to build one of the greatest mansions in the region. The house, located at 5500 North Washington in Denver, was made of brick and cut stone, featuring a grandiose Victorian cupola, with an interior of ten rooms with black walnut panels. The windows were French and the marble Italian.[226]

Shortly after the mansion was completed in 1873, however, Hindry's successes took a turn for the worse. His wife died, and his children moved away. Now alone in his palatial estate, Hindry was met with less than desirable neighbors. A smelting factory was made nearby, and the fumes and smoke from it killed the plants and filled his acreage with stinking fumes. Hindry filed a suit against the smelting company but lost.[227]

Rumors began to circulate that Hindry hid treasure in his house, which lured smelter workers to his property. Noticing these burglars, Hindry devised a shotgun trap by a window that was being used to break into his estate. On September 18, 1901, Hindry returned to find a dead man in his yard, shot through the chest with his rigged shotgun. This did not deter intruders, as two more were shot. This trap proved to be Hindry's own downfall, as one night after hearing what he thought to be more burglars, he tripped and was shot in the side. Despite surviving the ordeal, he moved to California in 1906, abandoning the house. It was at this time that rumors of the house being haunted began, either by Hindry himself or the ghosts of those that were shot there.[228]

In 1921, the house was purchased by one Leo Bomareto. Although the 1948 *Rocky Mountain News* article is the greatest resource for the biographical data of both Hindry and the house itself, its reputation as being haunted was evidently established by 1923. The house was leased by the city as an isolation hospital in 1923 to quarantine for malignant diseases. The article's title reads "Notorious 'Haunted House' Is Leased by Denver for Isolation Hospital." It details how the house was once a "gathering place for earlyday society," but that after "the Hindry family moved away for years the place was deserted, gradually assuming a reputation for harboring evil spirits."[229]

As mentioned, Dale Bailey's *American Nightmares: The Haunted House in American Popular Fiction* identifies what he calls the "formula for the haunted house tale."[230] The formula is essentially a structure that Bailey identified in haunted house stories, which includes an aristocratic house haunted by the supernatural, a family that moves has troubling encounters, a dual plot of physical and psychological isolation as the provenance of the haunting is discovered and a climax involving either the escape of the family or a twist establishing the recurring nature of evil. These stories often deal with themes such as race, class and gender conflicts; the clash between science and the supernatural; and a Manichean battle of good and evil.[231]

Although Bailey's formula focuses on haunted houses in popular fiction, many of these motifs and themes appear in the oral tradition related to the Hindry House. The setting is crucial to the haunted house formula. The Hindry House has an unsettling history because of the three burglars shot on the premises, and its name is derived from its eponymous aristocratic owner.

The plot Bailey identifies is similar to what happened with the Hindry family. However, instead of supernatural occurrences leading to psychological and physical isolation, they were inverted, as Hindry's isolation was in many ways what gave way to the haunting rumors. The climax of the story also results in Hindry abandoning the house and its ultimate destruction. Thematically, class struggles are the overarching focus of the Hindry saga. It was Hindry's position of wealth that led him to build such an audacious mansion in the first place, but ironically, it was his disenfranchisement in the face of an industry moving in that led to his demise.

BRADMAR

In the class that I taught at Pennsylvania State University about the history of monsters and the supernatural, I took my students to a house blocks away from campus that has gained the reputation of being haunted. The house was the location of a grisly triple murder on Christmas some years ago. After the subsequent arrest of the owner, the house was abandoned, and while it was abandoned, locals spread word of it being haunted. A similar abandoned-to-haunted trajectory occurred in one of Denver's haunted mansions: Bradmar.

Located at 4100 South University Boulevard, the house was built in 1919 when George W. Gano, president of a clothing company, commissioned it. The house is built in a magnificent Tudor style. George died in 1930, and his widow, Ethel, continued to live there until 1960. After her death, the house was vacant for ten months and was vandalized often. In May 1962, however, Dr. Robert Bradley and Dorothy (born Bomar) bought the home and decided to call it "Bradmar," a portmanteau of their names. Dr. Bradley was a member of the Academy of Parapsychology and Medicine and held fortnightly séances with mediums, and shortly after they moved in, the couple reported strange encounters at the house.[232]

In 1967, the Bradleys published a book called *Psychic Phenomena: Revelations and Experiences.* In the book, which features chapters on psychokinesis, reincarnation, hypnosis and faith healing, the Bradleys detail some of their own paranormal experiences at Bradmar. They recount hearing strange, disembodied footprints as well as experiencing mysterious electricity. One night, Karl, an interior designer, "heard footsteps proceeding through the lower floor of the house. It sounded as if they were made by someone in soft slippers....There was a pause. Then the steps proceeded back through the house....Finally, he again heard the slamming of the back door."[233] Although Karl heard these footprints, they were not made by anyone discernible.

Over the next two decades, Bradmar became known for its reputation as being haunted, something that the Bradleys did not shy away from. News articles started to appear about the Bradleys' experiences. In 1971, a *Rocky Mountain News* article included Dorothy expressing her belief that a poltergeist occupied the home; in 1976, Dr. Bradley jokingly said that the spirits are helpful and will pull down window shades when it is too bright; a 1971 *Rocky Mountain News* article said that Dr. Bradley witnessed a floating cigar case; and in 1979, a reporter at *Rocky Mountain News* saw the lights flicker on and off after expressing disappointment at the lack of parapsychological experiences. When the Bradleys decided to put the house for sale in 1972, the *Rocky Mountain News* proudly claimed the house had a resident ghost.[234]

The Bradleys had a unique response to their house being haunted. As parapsychologists, they clearly had an interest in the topic. One might imagine that they let their zeal for all things paranormal color their interpretations for subjective experiences such as footsteps and electric malfunctions. As Sylvia Ann Grider notes, the hauntings described in oral narratives are often more subdued than the over-the-top, demonic hauntings of Hollywood. The experiences of the Bradleys are not altogether dissimilar from those experienced by my family. To write off the Bradleys' encounters as imaginary, however, would be to ignore the warning they provide at the beginning of *Psychic Phenomena*:

> *Seeking these truths for ourselves, we were made ever more aware that the academic parapsychologists tend to ignore the religious and spiritual aspects in their studies of the nature of man. They are so very afraid of destroying the image they have recently been trying to build up as men of science. In their over-zealousness to prove themselves they take the attitude that anything that cannot be repeated at our will is the mere product of a credulous mind or of charlatanism. We, however, feel that theirs is a limited and partial view with no possible hope of explaining the whole.*[235]

These are a few of the famous haunted mansions of Denver that meet the archetypal form of the haunted house. But this is by no means an exhaustive list. The Avery House in Fort Collins is said to be haunted by the ghost of William Avery, who was murdered by his wife with arsenic (motif E221, *dead spouse's malevolent return)*. A house at Nineteenth and Grant had several articles about its haunted reputation in Denver newspapers between 1902 and 1904. The Elmer Vidger home at 1228 South Pennsylvania Street was reported to be haunted, as was Jack Parker's house at 765 Oneida. A house at Tenth Street in Leadville is said to be haunted by the ghost of a child whose remains are rumored to be in the basement.[236] A house at 1739 East Thirteenth Avenue, which has since been torn down, was the inspiration for the movie *The Changeling*.[237] And there are assuredly innumerable more houses that exist only in the oral tradition of those who live in them.

While there certainly is an "archetypal" form of the haunted house, an image that we have received through literature and popular culture, the stereotypical haunted space of high towers, dark windows, towering columns and spiderwebs does not always meet the reality of houses that have a reputation of being haunted by their residents. This is something I know all too well, having grown up in a house that was thought by my family and our friends to be home to a morally ambiguous specter we chose to call "Dave." Scholarly investigations of the supernatural, and ghosts in particular, occupy a somewhat muddy place where the "truth" of the matter must be set aside. I am not here to say that the house *was* haunted or that it was *not* haunted. What I can say, though, is that visitors to the house routinely commented on the uncanny aura of the place. It was not infrequent for me or my brothers to have a friend over, only for them to ask what was wrong with the house, despite them not having any preconceptions over the house's haunted reputation.

The house in question sits on the border of Evergreen and Conifer. In fact, the road it is on is the delineation point between these two mountain communities. Perhaps it is this liminal location at a crossroads that provided the house with its ostensibly supernatural disposition. The house itself is nothing like the archetypal haunted house identified by Bailey. It had no towers or turrets; it sat not at the top of the hill but in the middle of it; it had large windows that in no way were dark and gloomy; and despite being a large and "nice" house, it was not visually a symbol of aristocratic opulence and excess that many haunted houses are.

In preparation for this book, I interviewed my immediate and extended families about their experiences at the house. What I found was astonishing. Not only did everyone have their own stories, or what a folklorist would classify as a "memorate"—that is, a personal experience narrative about the supernatural—but these narratives conformed with scholarly theories about "the usefulness of ghost stories" as well. One thing that stood out the most is *where* these narratives took place: The stories often focused on the basement, a common place for stories of hauntings, as well as the bathroom, which is a space identified by Jeannie Thomas as being an overlooked focal point for ghost narratives.[238] A second aspect of these narratives is that the hauntings are relatively benign in comparison to the dramatized hauntings typical to Hollywood films.

Let's start out with the location of these hauntings inside of the house itself. As mentioned, several of the stories my family shared focused on the bathroom. The folklorist Jeannie Thomas says that "bathroom ghost stories may be the most marginalized type of narrative in a genre that is already trivialized."[239] This is despite the fact that ghost stories about bathrooms show up both in traditional oral narrative, as well as in popular fiction such as *Harry Potter*'s Moaning Myrtle, *The Amityville Horror*'s haunted toilets and *The House of the Seven Gables*' invisibly flushing toilets, with the latter of these two blurring the lines between fiction and reality based on their role as popular culture icons *and* actual locations.

For Thomas, these stories transmit cultural meaning. The bathroom, Thomas says, is the place where we confront the unseen forces in our bodies as well as come to terms with bodily processes we might see as shameful:

> *This room and its associations may also evoke a sense of shame for some. We also can't escape confronting bodily processes and issues of health in the bathroom. A child who hasn't yet mastered basic bodily functions can find being in the bathroom frightening and surprising. Adults confront illness, aging, and mortality in bathrooms, which may generate fear, sadness, or despair. Given the vulnerability, shame, and fear that are experienced in the bathroom, it makes cultural sense that such an emotionally charged space could become a common locale for hauntings.*[240]

If the bathroom is a space that is quite literally haunted by stories of ghosts, then why do we not associate them with the traditional spaces of the haunted house? The answer, Thomas suggests, is that because we don't usually connect the bathroom with traditional haunted iconography, we tend to overlook these stories, which can tell us not only about our ideas about the supernatural but also about the hidden processes of our bodies that we have anxiety about.

The first person in my family to share their story about the haunted bathroom in my childhood home was my cousin Critter, who said, "The biggest one [story] I had was in the bathroom. I was in there and lights just turned off out of nowhere and I got sketched out."

A second story came from Emma, who said, "I once got locked in the bathroom at the top of the stairs thinking it was the boys, but it wasn't." Though these stories are fairly benign, it is telling that they both took place in the bathroom, the liminal space identified by Thomas as the unclean part of the house where we clean ourselves and perform "ritually impure acts."[241]

While these bathroom stories were an idiosyncratic and intriguing part of my family's stories, they were by no means the only ones. My aunt told of seeing a full-bodied apparition that looked like my grandpa appear from out of the basement; my dad reported doors being slammed as we finally moved out of the house; my mom said a disembodied voice whispered in her ear, convincing her of the uncanniness of the house that she had been reluctant to accept; another cousin described a feeling of unease and the sensing of a presence when entering the house; finally, I shared my story of hearing footsteps walk up to my bedroom door, only to open it to see nobody there. All this in a house that does not meet the archetypal form.

CONCLUSION

When studying supernatural folklore, especially from an academic and scholarly perspective, one thing becomes abundantly clear: there is a tension between experience and culture that is always mediating our understanding of why places are haunted and what importance they have. I don't want to denigrate people's actual experiences that contribute to the reputations of places as being haunted. Oral tradition is full of personal experience narratives that speak of encounters with the supernatural and mysterious forces at haunted houses. In that way, a haunted place is reputed as such because of experience, but there are also clearly important cultural meanings projected onto these locations. It is no mistake that haunted houses are often not just houses but mansions. They are places that belong to the elite, venues that the common folk are excluded from. It is no surprise that they fill those mysterious, off-limits places with legends. This includes stories about infant mortality, fears about liminal spaces of the house such as the basement and staircases, specters of the Civil War and formulaic stories about spectral animals. My conclusion is that stories of hauntings are often an interplay of both experience and culture, but if you are brave enough to visit these houses, perhaps you can decide for yourself.

7
ON THE ROAD AGAIN

RIVERDALE ROAD

I am a haunted man.
—*Charles Harper*

Picture the following scenario: you've just turned eighteen, and you're transitioning from your years as an adolescent into being a full adult. You recently got a car and are using it to explore parts of your local town that were previously off-limits when you needed your parents to drive you there. You and your friends meet up with some girls, who tell you about a haunted road a few miles away. "This place is really haunted," they assure you, "a guy went crazy there and burned his house down. His spirit still haunts the streets." You see a chance to show your bravado, so you take the opportunity and drive out to the haunted location. When you get there, you perform some rituals to test your bravery and see if the supernatural really exists. To your amazement, something really does happen. You're overcome with fear or at least the sensation that something is really there.

The scenario described above is a common occurrence across the country and even the world. It is what folklorists refer to as a "legend trip." During a legend trip, people take a journey to a haunted location, often perform rituals to test the supernatural and tell stories about their experiences after. Folklorists have also used the term *ostension* to analyze legend trips.[242] Ostension comes from the Latin "to show," and in folkloristics, the word has been used to describe acting out a legend instead of just describing it. As opposed to merely telling a story about a haunted road, this story can become an act of ostension by going on a legend trip to the location itself.

Folklorists have made several arguments for why legend trips are done in the first place. Bill Ellis argues that legend trips can be "rituals of rebellion."[243] He says that for adolescents, these legend trips can be mechanisms to escape adult supervision, to experiment with substances and sex and to perform rituals deemed antisocial. Another reason that legend trips might be popular is that they often occur at liminal life stages.[244] *Liminal* is a term used to describe aspects of our lives that are betwixt and between, neither fully here nor fully there. Legend trips may be popular for adolescents because they are in a transitional phase between being a child and an adult. Haunted roads are a perfect liminal space because they often lie at the margins of town, therefore becoming a great legend site.[245]

Legends themselves are ambiguous. A legend can be defined as a narrative that is set in historical place and historic time and is presented as being believable, with a strange and often supernatural element to it. Legends make claims about reality. The tales they tell are related as if they happened or could have happened, whether that is a maniac burning his house, a vanishing hitchhiker or stories about sacrificial killings.

One place in Colorado incorporates all of these legend and more. Riverdale Road, an eleven-mile stretch between Brighton and Thornton just north of Denver, has been called one of the most haunted roads in the country. Legends seem to find a natural resting place at Riverdale Road. Here, there are stories about a man who burned his family alive in their mansion after going insane, and they say the ghost of his wife still roams the streets as a "lady in white," and there are tales about a haunted chicken coop from their property. Legends say that there is a place in Riverdale Road called "Jogger's Hill," where a ghost will tap on your car before disappearing, as well as a Phantom Camaro that shows up on this sinuous road that has been home to a number of real-life vehicular deaths.[246] There are stories about a haunted tree that was used to hang slaves and even stories of hellhounds.

Each of these legends are what folklorists refer to as "migratory legends," which are legends that keep a similar form but shape themselves for different areas that they find expression in.[247] Stories about men going crazy and burning their houses, phantom joggers or spectral hounds are not unique to Riverdale Road. They are narratives that express some vital piece of cultural information and have chosen the language of legends to articulate them. This is not to say they don't carry significant meaning—in fact, quite the opposite.

Riverdale Road. *Photo by author.*

Legends, and in this case, legends about haunted roads, are, as the folklorist Thomas White puts it, "localized manifestations of larger cultural scares."[248] In short, they are trying to speak about a cultural taboo that we might struggle to articulate.

Let us return to the example of a legend trip that I provided at the beginning of this chapter. This was a fairly generic narrative of what a legend trip might look like. Adolescents use a car to travel to a haunted road in order to impress some girls; they test the supernatural through ritual, ostensive acts; and then, to their amazement, actually encounter something in the process. While this was a fairly stock example of a legend trip, it matches identically with a memorate, or personal experience narrative with a supernatural element, that I documented. I spoke with a paranormal investigator named Jonathan Keyworth, who told me the following story about his legend trip to Riverdale Road as a teenager nearly thirty years ago.

> *Jonathan: Me and my buddy, we were up in Thornton, and we were at a country bar.... We were dancing and stuff and we met these girls, and they were like, "Have you ever been to Riverdale Road?" I was like, "No, what the hell is that?" And they're like, "Well the ghost runs right by you..." I was like "OK, let's prove it...." So we drove out there, I was driving too, and there was no alcohol, I was eighteen at the time....So there was no intoxication, we were all sober. We got to Riverdale Road, and we got to this parking lot.... We got out of the car, and they told us to go to the northwest corner of the parking lot....I stood in this corner and they took thirty steps back, and I kid you not man, sure as shit, I hear these steps just like running, like jogging in the gravel. And it ran right by me, and I got extremely cold on the left side of my body, and once it ran by me it started over again, and there's nothing out there. I got scared and ran to the truck. I'm like, "If you want to go, get in the truck." So that's when I knew that spirit existed, was in Riverdale Road and that kind of opened my mind.*

Jonathan's narrative fits in directly with the traditional shape of a legend trip. He and his buddy, eighteen at the time, met some girls and drove to a place with a haunted reputation. While there, they tested the supernatural through ritual. In Jonathan's case, he actually had an experience there that influenced him throughout the course of his life and opened his mind to the possibility of the supernatural.

THE DAVID WOLPERT HOUSE

Many of the legends that circulate about Riverdale Road seem to have a nexus from which all the other legends arise. This origin point is the legend of a man who went crazy and burned his entire family alive. A typical version of this legend goes like this:

> *Those courageous enough to travel through the Gates of Hell come upon the ruins of the old mansion. It is said that the man that built it lost his mind. One night, he set the entire mansion ablaze with his wife and children asleep inside before he disappeared, never to be held accountable. Muffled screams can be heard echoing against these now crumbling walls that bared witness to the unspeakable crime.…What people really come to see is what was once an underground chicken coop where mysterious markings cover the walls. It is said that it was here that the mansion's builder, prior to slaughtering his family, would conjure spirits and demons. Hidden from sight beneath the ground, he wrote symbols of black magic on the walls in the blood of his victims, trying to access power from an unseen world.*[249]

The legend of the burned mansion has several defining features. First, it tells of a man who lost his mind and, as a result, burned his house down with his family inside. Importantly, he disappeared, never to be seen again. Second, it's said that the unnamed murderer practiced black magic and that he used part of his property to conjure spirits. The legend says that there are residuals of these practices, in that the legendary white lady of Riverdale Road is thought to be his wife and that the chicken coop is still haunted by the energy that lingers there. Most importantly, however, is that these legends are not tied to any specific historic events or people. Beyond that, they are not idiosyncratic to Colorado, much less Thornton, but instead are regional expressions of more recognizable legend types.

Let's start with the mansion itself. You may notice that the owner of the mansion is not named during the legend narrative. According to Katie Rudolph, an archivist and librarian at the Denver Public Library, there was a catastrophic mansion fire on Riverdale Road.[250] On November 28, 1975, a house at 9190 Riverdale Road burned down. The fire was significant enough that *The Denver Post* ran a story about it. The house was called the Wolpert Mansion, named after a gold prospector named David Wolpert who came to Colorado in the 1850s and made his living in farming. The fire was preceded by the burning of a chicken coop on the property, consistent with the legend. As Rudolph notes, the chicken coop burning was accompanied by vandalism, which may explain legends about Satanism and conjuration, and she cites a passage from *The Forgotten Past of Adams County, Volume 1*:

> *In May 1975, when the chicken house burned down, the fire department came and extinguished the fire and put in a report to county health authorities stating that the house was a fire hazard and a danger to the community. The health department ordered the owner to dismiss the tenants. When they moved, heavy vandalism started.*[251]

The crux of this legend, that of a man going crazy and burning his family alive, is not found solely in Colorado. One thing folklorists have done is compile bits of folklore, or motifs, into indexes in hopes to classify them and to be able to identify aspects of traditional storytelling. One such index is Stith Thompson's *Motif-Index of Folk-Literature*, which includes motif S112.0.2 *House burned with all inside*.[252] The story of the Wolpert Mansion clearly falls under this motif category.

The story of the Wolpert Mansion is also similar to two other popular legends: Char-Man and the Cropsey Maniac. Char-Man is a legend that stems from the Ojai Valley in California. In a standard variant of the legend, a fire consumes Ojai Valley, and in one house a son is driven crazy by the events, hangs his father (who died in the fire) by his feet, skins him and disappears, only to haunt the area of Old Creek Road with his charred face from the fire (from which the name Char-Man originates).[253] Another aspect of the Riverdale Road legends are stories of a haunted tree. This story also tells of a devastating house fire that kills a family, with the survivor escaping, and also concentrates on the road that the legend takes place in.

The Cropsey Maniac is another closely related legend. As is the case with most legends, if not all legends, there are multiple variants of the

Cropsey story. A standard version tells of a man named Cropsey, who was an upstanding citizen with a vacation house near a summer camp in New York State. He sends his wife and children there a few days before he intends on leaving, and in the meantime they die in a devastating house fire. Cropsey reacts pathologically and seeks revenge on the campers, whom he sees as responsible for the deaths.[254] In the case of Char-Man and Cropsey, the survivors go crazy after the fire, and it is the deaths of their family members that drive them crazy, whereas the Wolpert Mansion legends are the opposite. In all cases, however, the survivor escapes and haunts the area.

What are we supposed to do with these legends? Clearly they are trying to tell us something. In the legend of the Wolpert Mansion, it seems to be expressing larger societal fears while using Riverdale Road as a local, regional point to do so, as opposed to expressing specifically Colorado fears and anxieties through a recognizable tale type. The story of this burned mansion articulates fears about those we keep closest to us. It gives a language to express the anxiety that even those who we trust the most might turn evil and become our worst enemies. When this happens, the house, which should be our sanctuary, becomes a final resting place.

THE PHANTOM JOGGER

As Riverdale Road runs through a neighborhood, it is no surprise that legends express fears about domestic life. It is even less surprising that the other legends from the road are about the precarity of the road itself. One of the most famous legends from Riverdale Road is the Phantom Jogger. The basic form this legend usually takes is that a jogger died on Riverdale Road after being hit by a car. The driver panicked and left the jogger for dead, causing the jogger to haunt the hill in the afterlife. If you go to "Jogger's Hill," the place where the jogger died, and park your car, you might experience the sensation that you are being pulled to the side of the road. While your car is stopped, you might hear them coming toward you, and after the ordeal is over, there will be handprints on the car to show they were there. This compelling legend is a localized pastiche of two well-known urban legends: the Vanishing Hitchhiker and what Carl Lindahl calls a "gravity hill." A common version of the legend goes like this:

> *If you pull over near an area known as Jogger's Hill you may run into an angry spirit looking to take revenge. Many drivers have reported being forced to pull to the side of the road when their car mysteriously begins to fail, attempting to lurch forward before it finally dies. If you're silent enough you'll start to hear the sounds of a set of rushing footsteps approaching. Only seconds later a handprint will appear on your windshield before a violent pounding of ghostly fists slams onto the sides of your car. The story goes that there once was a jogger who went out for a nighttime run. Around one of the bends, a speeding car raced down, not paying attention, and hit the jogger. The unknown car pulled over for just a moment as the jogger lay dying, begging for help only for his calls to be ignored as the driver sped off. The jogger's spirit is said to wander Jogger's Hill looking for his killer. When a car stops on the road the jogger rushes to the car and places his hands on the windows to get a look at the driver before beating the car in frustration.*[255]

This version shows some of the defining characteristics of the Phantom Jogger. A person has died after being hit by a car on Riverdale Road, and they are now looking for revenge. While you are parked, the phantom tries to get to the driver's side window to get a look at the person who killed them. Importantly, a handprint is left on the car, showing their presence, but they disappear after.

Stories about phantoms on the side of the road conjure visions of one of the most famous urban legends: the Vanishing Hitchhiker. Legends about the Vanishing Hitchhiker have been documented by folklorists since the 1940s, and it was made famous by Jan Harold Brunvand in his 1981 book *The Vanishing Hitchhiker: American Urban Legends and Their Meanings*. Like the Phantom Jogger, the Vanishing Hitchhiker (which is at times called the Phantom Hitchhiker) tells of a phantom seen on the side of the road who is often picked up by the driver, only to disappear during the drive. Often, the driver learns after the fact that the hitchhiker was the ghost of a recently deceased individual who died under unfortunate or unexpected circumstances.

Legend scholars Gillian Bennett and Paul Smith provide an overview of the basic structure of the Vanishing Hitchhiker:

> *The central story is that a motorist gives a ride to a stranded traveler who mysteriously disappears from the vehicle and is later discovered to be an other world personage of some sort—a ghost, alien, prophet, or sacred personage.*

> *If the hitchhiker is a ghost, he/she may be picked up outside a cemetery or an isolated road. He/she is usually trying to get to a particular destination, most often his/her home or a party. If the hitchhiker is a girl she may conduct a romance with the driver, who only later discovers he has been making love to a ghost. The story will end with the ghostlines of the hitchhiker being established in some way. This may be some sort of evidence being left in the car or on a grave.*[256]

The Phantom Jogger is clearly a Colorado version of the Vanishing Hitchhiker. Both tell of an apparition on the side of the road who is later revealed as being a specific individual, and evidence is left of their presence. As with all folklore, it takes on its own idiosyncratic variations to match its specific cultural context. What better way for Colorado, a state famous for its physical fitness, to have a Vanishing Hitchhiker legend about a jogger.

A specific feature of the Phantom Jogger that connects it to other, lesser-known legends is the place of the legend itself, Jogger's Hill, and the handprints left on the car. Folklorists Carl Lindahl and Jeannie Thomas

Riverdale Road looking north. *Photo by author.*

have written about their experiences at San Antonio's "gravity hill," where legends say that a train killed a busload of children and that they still haunt the location. If you go to the legend site, you might experience the sensation that you are moving uphill when you are really going downhill. When you get out of the car, you will see handprints on your car, which marks the presence of the ghostly children, who have been pushing your car.[257] This legend is very similar to Jogger's Hill. Both tell of gravitational anomalies experienced in a car and handprints left by the ghostly assailants. To my knowledge, this legend type doesn't have an official name, but I suggest "gravity hill" is as good a name as any. These legends together articulate a very real fear: that of being killed in an automobile accident.

The Lady in White and the Phantom Camaro

Two of the other most famous (or infamous) legends from Riverdale Road are intertwined with both the David Wolpert House and the dangers of the road itself. These are the Lady in White and the Phantom Camaro, which, like the preceding legends, share the common theme of death. And like the other stories from Riverdale Road, they also incorporate noticeable motifs from traditional folklore to make them more recognizable and tellable.

The legend of the Lady in White holds that visitors to Riverdale Road might notice a woman clad in white garments walking on the side of the road. When you look into your rearview mirror, she will be gone. Some internet blogs suggest that the Lady in White is the deceased wife of the man who burned down his mansion:

> *Witnesses report that a lady in white walks the road by the gates. Assumed to be his wife, she searches the street for her murdered children or even her husband. She might be out for revenge, but the most she's ever done to visitors is appear in the rearview mirror as they pass by, longing for help that never comes.*[258]

For many, the stories of the burned mansion and the Lady in White are intertwined.

When looking at the legend of the Lady in White, it might be apparent that it is similar to the Vanishing Hitchhiker. In fact, stories about Ladies in White are often cited in folklore literature as examples of the Vanishing

Hitchhiker. Take for example the following legend from Gillian Bennett and Paul Smith's compendium *Urban Legends*:

> *The White Lady of Longnor comes out of the Black Pool, and flits about the roads. She was disappointed in love, rural gossips say, and so perambulates at the old trysting time, in hope to meet her faithless swain once more.*[259]

This version comes all the way from England, yet it is remarkably similar to the Lady in White as we know her in Thornton, Colorado. Both of these figures are not only clad in white but also searching in the afterlife for their lover, one hoping for revenge, the other for reciprocated love.

Another famous legend from Riverdale Road is known as the Phantom Camaro. This legend says that a driver died on Riverdale Road in the 1970s after meeting their demise on one of the road's dangerous blind corners. A common version of the story goes like this:

> *One driver in the 70s was zipping down the road, impatiently testing fate with their gas pedal, when they had a fatal crash. Now if you drive down the street during the night or day, a phantom Camaro with one working headlight might pull up behind you, challenging you to a race with no happy ending.*[260]

The Ghost Car is a common motif in both folklore and popular culture. Stephen King's novel *Christine*, published in 1983, tells of a car possessed by malevolent forces. It is unclear when stories about the Phantom Camaro began, but they are similar in period to King's book. There are stories across the world of cars taking a spectral form or being owned by dead people who inhabit the car, such as Russia's Black Volga.[261]

CONCLUSION

Stories about death on the road and in the houses that populate Riverdale Road are no surprise. The road itself is a dangerous place, as Colorado's icy and snow-packed roads often are. In recent memory, there have been numerous fatal crashes on the road because of the winding nature of the thoroughfare.[262] But there is something symbolic about the road itself.

As Thomas White notes, the road symbolizes a journey, and places like Riverdale Road symbolize the path towards the supernatural.[263] This is one reason why legend trippers like those I interviewed find a haunted road an apt place for them to test the supernatural. The historic and dramatic fire of the David Wolpert House inspired many of the legends that take place at Riverdale Road. Although there were no deaths like legends of the White Lady suggest, nor were there Satanic rituals in the chicken coop, an event like that is bound to inspire legends. As is the case with most folklore, we'll likely never know exactly how and when these legends began to circulate. What is clear, though, is that they are regional adaptations of stories that span the world over. In that sense, Riverdale Road is our conduit, our bridge, to the wider world of lore and storytelling.

8
SPECTERS OF PARKS

HAUNTED PLACES

All work and no play makes Jack a dull boy
—The Shining

Where are you most likely to encounter a ghost? At a haunted road? In a haunted house? In truth, legends of hauntings occur in a great variety of locations. A major premise of this book has been that hauntings originate in liminal spaces, places that are either spatially or temporally "betwixt and between." Another key idea of this volume is that the supernatural is often hidden in plain sight, and traditions of legends can be found in much more locations than one might think. To list out every haunted location in Colorado would take several volumes spanning thousands of pages.

Instead of listing out every location and providing brief codas on the lore of the place, in this chapter I focus on three types of haunted locations as they appear in Colorado: hotels, cemeteries and bridges. Each of these locations are liminal spaces that inspire legendry. Hotels are places that are marked by ephemerality. They are locations where people check in for a brief stay and leave shortly after. As the famous *Eagles* song specifies, however, ghosts at hotels can check out any time they like, but they might never leave. Bridges are famous spots for hauntings. They are neither a road, nor not a road, as they connect one area to the next. Cemeteries are by their very nature liminal. They are the very point of contact between the living and the dead. Unsurprisingly, they inspire legends of hauntings all over the Centennial State.

Each section of this chapter focuses on one of these themes by putting them in context with theoretical approaches to understand why legends of these places exist. Once again, we find ourselves bound between the Scylla and Charybdis of legend research: experience and culture. There are reasons why these specific places inspire legends, but those legends can also be rooted in phenomenological experience. In other words, while a cemetery is the ideal liminal space for a legend complex, stories of hauntings at these locations can be inspired by personal experience at the location.

THE STANLEY HOTEL

Of all the locations associated with hauntings, the hotel might be the most common. In researching for this chapter, I accumulated a huge list of hotels in Colorado that are reputed as haunted. This includes the Hotel Colorado, the Broadmoor Hotel, the Palace Hotel and Casino, the Hotel Boulderado, the Brown Palace Hotel, the Oxford Hotel, the Hotel Teatro, the Homestead Motel, the Newhouse Hotel, the Hotel Jerome, the View Hotel and the Brook Forest Inn, and most notably, the Stanley Hotel. While this is a list

The Stanley Hotel. *Photo by author.*

of some of the most notable haunted Colorado hotels, I am sure there are more. To merely list them out and talk about their associated lore would be, I think, a bit redundant. Instead, I will focus on Colorado's most infamous hotel: the Stanley Hotel in Estes Park.

First, we must ask ourselves why hotels are thought to be haunted in the first place. As Dianne Goldstein notes, hotels are "intricately linked to symbolic events typically associated with reasons for ghostly return—marriages, acts of infidelity, and natural deaths."[264] The choice for hotels to decide whether or not they will capitalize on the haunted reputation poses an interesting choice for hotel management. Do you risk becoming associated with the supernatural and seek to capitalize on that reputation through playing into the reputation? That can often be a lucrative decision. Such is the case with Colorado's Stanley Hotel. Or, do you avoid such associations and attempt to ignore the rumors of hauntings at the hotel? The tendency of the former is what Dianne Goldstein has called "the commodification of belief,[265] in that places like hotels can turn vernacular belief into a commodified form, where the interplay between beliefs about haunted locations and a financial capitalization on them are intertwined. In Colorado, there is no better place to study this than the Stanley Hotel in Estes Park.

Estes Park from Stanley Hotel. *Photo by author.*

The Stanley Hotel has been renowned as one of Colorado's most luxurious hotels since it opened in 1909. It sits high on the hills overlooking Estes Park, a somewhat remote town about an hour's drive from Boulder. As you make your descent into Estes Park, the craggy rocks of the mountains capture your eye, but after you take in the marvelous mountain landscape, the alluring white façade of the Stanley Hotel announces itself as the true centerpiece of the town. In preparation for this chapter, I visited the Stanley Hotel myself and attended *The Shining* ghost tour of the hotel. Much of what follows comes from my field notes from this tour.

Estes Park was first settled in the 1870s when Windham Thomas Wyndham-Quin, the 4th Earl of Dunraven, came to the region in hopes of finding a place for big game hunting. The earl claimed fifteen thousand acres for himself, though his claims were disputed. Shortly after, Freelan Oscar Stanley, one of the inventors of the popular Stanley steam cars, known by his friends as F.O., came to Estes Park to battle consumption. Stanley came to the region hoping to live his remaining years peacefully, but the mountain air invigorated him and his consumption receded. He and his wife decided to build a hotel in Estes Park so other wealthy patrons could visit. In 1909, the Stanley Hotel opened, and it quickly became a destination for many elite guests, including the unsinkable Molly Brown, who enjoyed transgressing gendered boundaries and would drink to excess in the Pinon Room, a billiard and drinking lounge usually reserved for male patrons.

The Earl of Dunraven at the Stanley Hotel. *Photo by author.*

The early haunted legacy of the Stanley Hotel may be traced back to F.O. Stanley's wife, Flora, who had an interest in spiritualism, and would routinely hold séances on the grounds. However, after the hotel's golden age passed, it fell into disrepair and gained a reputation as being haunted.[266] One of these legends involves Flora, as guests have reported hearing the 1909 Steinway piano she loved being played by an invisible force.

The legacy of the Stanley Hotel changed dramatically in 1974 when

Left: The 1909 Steinway Piano at the Stanley Hotel. *Photo by author.*

Right: The balcony of Room 217, where Stephen King conceived of *The Shining*. *Photo by author.*

Stephen King visited. King was staying in room 217 at the Stanley when he had a terrible nightmare of his son being chased by one of the fire hoses at the hotel. He awoke the next morning, stood on the balcony of the room and had the story of *The Shining* come to him. *The Shining* tells the story of the character Jack Torrance, who comes to the Overlook Hotel, which was inspired by the Stanley, his descent into madness, encounters with spectral hotel patrons and his attempt to murder his wife and child. The book was ultimately turned into a movie by Stanley Kubrick, which King reviled for its creative differences, and a miniseries overseen by King was shot on the hotel's grounds.

The publication of King's novel and the subsequent adaptations of it led to a complete reversal of the hotel's fortunes. Where it was once in disrepair, massive reconstruction efforts went into restoring the hotel. The Stanley has decided to lean in heavily into this reputation, offering daily tours that focus on the hotel's history, its connection to *The Shining* and its ghost legends. This has led, of course, to a heavy commodification of these legends, but there are also notable experientially generated narratives at the hotel.

Aside from the spectral piano player, guests have reported seeing ghostly children running around the Concert Hall and the Pinon Room. One notorious legend centers on a specter known as "Dennis the Menace," a shadow figure reported to have glowing eyes. Dennis is reported to enjoy Dum-Dum lollipops, and a viral video taken by a tour guest shows an invisible force manipulating a Dum-Dum stick.[267] Astonishingly, at the tour I went to, the person sitting next to me had packed a Dum-Dum in her purse for the day. Another popular legend is that the hotel is haunted by Elizabeth Wilson, a housekeeper who was injured in an explosion in the ballroom in 1911. The hotel's disrepair during the mid-twentieth century has also inspired haunting legends, as it is said the ghost of a homeless squatter named Lucy haunts the grounds. In *The Shining*, the concert hall is the space where the past keeps playing itself out, and that is the case at the hotel as well, as rumors say a worker named Paul haunts it and enforces the hotel's curfews. Finally, there are stories about a specter called the "Stinky Man," who is known for his pungent aroma.[268]

The cultural theorist Mark Fisher has brilliantly interpreted Stanley Kubrick's adaptation of *The Shining* as being hauntological. Hauntology, as covered in previous chapters, is the notion that we are haunted by imagined pasts and aborted futures. "Haunting," Fisher says, "can be seen as intrinsically resistant to the contraction and homogenization of time and space. It happens when a place is stained by time, or when a particular place becomes the site for an encounter with broken time."[269] The Stanley Hotel is the place where this contraction has occurred, where "time is out of joint," to use the language of Hamlet and Derrida, and where the ghosts of the past keep repeating into the present. The legends of the Stanley tell us about the history of the hotel itself, of the mistreatment of workers and of the plights of the homeless. *The Shining*, Fisher says, is consumed with anxieties about the emergence of tele-technologies, which "is the form contemporary power increasingly assumes."[270] Fisher was writing in 2012, but this is even more true today, where corporate power is exerted through endless strings of telepresences in the form of monotonous Zoom meetings and endless email chains. Is there anything more dystopian than corporate overlords tracking keyboard strokes?

Another brilliant exegesis of *The Shining* comes from the documentary *Room 237*. The documentary interprets Kubrick's film as being about historical tragedies that continue to haunt us into the present, including the Native American genocide, the Holocaust and darker aspects of Colorado's history such as the cannibalistic Donner party and its intertwined legacy with westward expansion and therefore Manifest Destiny. These readings come from close readings of the film's mise-en-scène, such as the presence of Calumet baking powder tins and the Nazi-era typewriter that Jack hammers away at. Though these are the ways the Stanley has been portrayed in popular culture instead of the oral tradition, as the authors of *Haunting Experiences* have demonstrated, these two seemingly opposing ends of "culture" are often intertwined.[271] Such is the case at the Stanley Hotel. The connection between popular culture and folklore has recently been described by Jeffrey Tolbert and Michael Dylan Foster as a Möbius strip, a feedback loop where folklore informs popular culture and vice versa.[272] At the Stanley Hotel, folklore and popular culture continually influence each other, and this can be seen quite clearly through the haunted tours where the line between oral tradition and the influence of *The Shining*, both the movie and the novel, blurs.

Room 237 replica at the Stanley Hotel. *Photo by author.*

THE THIRD BRIDGE

Outside of Bennett, a small town of just over two thousand, sits one of Colorado's most legendary locations: the Third Bridge. This bridge, which lies on the expansive County Line Road, is home to many legends, including stories about spectral drums and ghost men riding astride phantom horses. Once again, we must ask ourselves why bridges are so commonly associated with hauntings. Crucially, bridges exhibit that defining trait of liminality that is so often tied to stories about the supernatural. Bridges are liminal spaces that are betwixt and between one area and the next. That in-betweenness and ambiguity often incite stories about hauntings. As we covered in the Riverdale Road chapter, roads themselves evoke an ethos of a journey to the afterlife, especially when they are tied to fatal car accidents, as is the case at the Third Bridge.

Legends and myths about bridges are not unique to Colorado. This is where European folklore says one is most likely to encounter trolls. In Norse mythology, the Bifröst is the rainbow bridge that connects Midgard, the realm of the mortals, to Asgard, the realm of the gods. In Zoroastrianism, bridges are also reminiscent of the connection between life and death, as the Chinvat Bridge is thought in that ancient monotheistic religion to separate the realm of the living from the realm of the dead. The Aarne-Thompson-Uther identifies the motif "The Devil's Bridge" as ATU 1191.[273] In Denton, Texas, the Old Alton Bridge is also known as "Goatman's Bridge" and is said to be home to a terrifying entity known as the Goatman. All of these legends indicate that the liminality of the bridge evokes a sense of connection between life and death, of the natural and the supernatural.

Inevitably, the concreteness of the bridge's location often inspires legend trips. This was observed by Linda Dégh in her early studies of bridge legends. Dégh says, "The stories in the bridge legends cluster…have two distinct parts. The first recounts a supernatural (or extraordinary) event that occurred in the past and that serves as an explanation of a present phenomenon attributed to it."[274] The second part, Elizabeth Tucker explains, "includes an account of the active and real physical participation on the part of the narrator and his associates."[275] In other words, there are two parts to the bridge legend: explanations for why the bridge is haunted in the first place and narratives of legend trippers to the location. At the Third Bridge, there are specific reasons for its haunted reputation that typify why it has gone through Colorado ecotypification as well as numerous memorates shared by legend trippers on online fora.

Legends about the Third Bridge focus on three specific historical occurrences to explain why the bridge is haunted in the first place: the Sand Creek Massacre, the Hungate Massacre and car accidents. The Sand Creek Massacre is certainly one of the darkest moments in Colorado's history. During the 1860s, ongoing negotiations between Colorado's politicians and the local American Indian tribes resulted in a fragile peace between the two. On November 29, 1864, however, Colonel Chivington assembled troops and attacked an American Indian camp at Sand Creek, which resulted in the deaths of many innocent Natives, including women and children.[276] One of the most common legends at the Third Bridge is that when you visit there, you will hear the sound of Native American drums beating in the distance. However, there is no clear connection between The Third Bridge and the Sand Creek Massacre site, which is a two-and-a-half-hour drive southeast of the bridge outside the small town of Eads. Still, the connection between the legend and the massacre speaks to the way this dark Colorado event still lives in the public consciousness as a dark specter of our past.

A second explanation for the hauntings at the Third Bridge is the Hungate Massacre, which was "a precipitating factor leading to the Sand Creek Massacre."[277] In 1861, the Treaty of Fort Wise was signed, which stipulated that the American Indian tribes would limit their hunting, relocate and be provided with provisions in exchange for crops. However, crop failures occurred and the government did not honor their end of the treaty. This, coupled with Governor John Evans's call for the murder of Cheyenne Indians, led to retaliatory raids. On the morning of June 11, 1864, Nathan Hungate, a rancher near the town of Elizabeth, set out with one Mr. Miller looking for cattle, when he saw smoke coming from the area near his cabin. When he returned, Hungate found his cabin on fire with his family killed. Miller rode to Denver with news of the massacre, and when they rode back, they found Hungate's body there as well.[278] The Hungate Massacre occurred far closer to the Third Bridge than did the Sand Creek Massacre, though the two are connected through the American Indian Wars of the 1860s, and both are connected to the legends of ghost drums (motif D1211) at the bridge.

A third explanation for the bridge being haunted comes from more contemporary events, specifically car accidents that have occurred there. Two specific crashes are cited as the impetus for these legends. In 1997, a car of teenagers lost control on the bridge and crashed into a creek, resulting in the death of two girls.[279] These girls are said to haunt the bridge, which Ernest Baughman identified as motif E332.1(a) "ghost appears at a bridge."[280] Nearly twenty years later, another fatal crash occurred in October 2016, when a car of five teenagers crashed after leaving the Third Bridge, with all of them dying.[281] Legends often have a specific purpose, which is to remind us of something. Elizabeth Tucker says there is a reason for the telling of a legend: "the communication of a message—a warning and/or advice of some kind."[282] At the Third Bridge, one of these messages is clearly the dangers of driving.

If there is one thing that folktales have taught us, it is that interdictions are meant to be violated. While the legends warn of the dangers of visiting the Third Bridge, inevitably legend trippers choose to travel there to test their bravery. Memorates, personal experience narratives of the supernatural, are often shared on online forums, and one Reddit user recounted their legend trip to the Third Bridge:

> *We hadn't been sitting there more than 2 min when I see, at the foot of the Bridge below us, a tall dark figure just standing there. I knew it was staring at us, you could feel it. It had no facial features it was just this solid black figure. You could tell it was a person though....As I return my focus back to this thing it started sprinting at us. Once it started running something was waving on this thing at about foot level, like it was wearing a damn cape. I put that SUV in reverse and got the hell out of there.*[283]

A common aspect of legend trips are details of meeting "uncanny persons or creatures" at the site,[284] and this memorate details how that is the case at the Third Bridge.

Other memorates attest to the haunted nature of the bridge. One individual recollected seeing a "ghost car" after being instructed not to go to the bridge because of the deaths that had occurred there:

> [We] *decided to go to the third bridge...and wanted to speed to the bridge as we almost there we got pulled over and the cop was yelling at us saying "do you guys not know what happened to the 4 boys who were up here speeding..." after the cop left we were about to get out the car and saw a car speeding on the opposite side of us then randomly disappeared.*[285]

This narrative demonstrates the connection between the legends and the car crashes that have occurred at the bridge and is reminiscent of the Phantom Camaro of Riverdale Road. Yet another memorate shows the connections between the bridge and stories about residual effects of the American Indian Wars:

> *We got a picture of a tall shadow figure when under the bridge....I saw a tall black figure behind a tree on the right side of the bridge....The ghosts ended up touching my friends sweatshirts and pulling on clothing. I heard branches snapping when we were on-top of the bridge and the drumming for a couple of seconds. I got a picture of something that looks like a skin-walker.*[286]

Ultimately, the legends of Colorado's Third Bridge speak to the state's dark past in connection to nineteenth-century massacres and contemporary car accidents while being a local version of the mythological motif of the magic bridge. Our very own Bifröst will likely continue to inspire visitors to test the boundaries of their bravery.

CHEESMAN PARK

To conclude this book, I return to a central idea that has permeated my discussions of the legends, ghosts and haunted histories contained herein: that folklore makes culture manifest. This idea is often overlooked by writers of local and regional folklore, and I hope that this book can inspire future authors to look at the context of folklore over the text. Professional folklorists know this all too well. To finalize our journey through the supernatural folklore through Colorado, we look at one of the most famous haunted locations in the state: Cheesman Park.

Though today Cheesman Park is frequented by locals looking for a good place to take a walk, to play with their dog or to enjoy a nice sunny day, it was originally a cemetery. While researching for this chapter, I uncovered legends of many cemeteries in the state, including Central City's Masonic Cemetery, the Mt. Pisgah Cemetery in Cripple Creek and Colorado Springs' Evergreen Cemetery. Typically, I would explain why a location such as this might inspire legends of hauntings. That might be less clear for a hotel or a bridge, but in the case of cemeteries I think this is fairly obvious. These are locations where death is confronted in no uncertain terms. The cemetery is a living memento mori. But why should death inspire haunted legends? If nothing else, it tells us about our own views of the afterlife. At Cheesman Park, however, there is a specific history that tells us about our own mores in regards to the treatment of the dead and the repercussions for when these taboos are violated.

When Denver was first founded in 1859, the area that is now Cheesman Park was used as the city's first cemetery, known officially as Prospect Hill Cemetery and colloquially as Mount Prospect. The area around Mount Prospect was developed rapidly after the establishment of a nearby area as the spot for the new capitol building. Many affluent people moved in, especially those who had grown rich from the gold and silver mining boom. However, the cemetery quickly became an eyesore, and the neighborhood petitioned for it to be turned into a park. The city agreed, and the city hired an undertaker, E.P. McGovern, to move the bodies to Riverside Cemetery.

McGovern was paid $1.90 for every box he moved, but he realized quickly that he could make his work easier. He and his comrades began to dismantle the bodies and stuff them into child-sized coffins. This macabre endeavor was quickly uncovered, and an article ran in the March 19, 1893 edition of *The Denver Republican* that detailed McGovern's sinister plot to

Cheesman Park. *Photo by author.*

dismember the bodies. The article says, "Comment is scarcely necessary on the above state of affairs. Beside the outrage offered to humanity in the method of dismembering the dead described above an opportunity is also offered to those connected with the work to swindle the city out of thousands of dollars."[287] Here we can see the way that folklore makes culture manifest. Desecration of bodies and improper burials are major cultural taboos. Since Homer's *Iliad*, when Achilles rode around the walls of Troy with the desecrated body of Hector, improper treatment of the body after death has been recorded as a cultural violation with major consequences. One of them is the idea that those spaces may be haunted. After McGovern's plot was uncovered, not all of the bodies were able to be moved. It is estimated that two thousand unmarked graves still exist at Cheesman Park.[288]

Today, Cheesman Park has gained a reputation as being haunted by those poor souls. Ghost tours are offered of the Capitol Hill area, with Cheesman being a major focal point because of its interesting history. This is an example of "dark tourism," where personal encounters with the macabre are offered. People have described sensations of fear and dread at the park, especially in cold spots that may indicate the presence of an unmarked grave. A mansion that existed in the Cheesman Park neighborhood that has since been torn down also served as the inspiration for the 1980 horror film *The Changeling*, indicating another instance of the recursive relationship between folklore and popular culture. In the end, Cheesman Park is a reminder of the lasting effects of our choices, and how what we do in the here and now has residual effects in the future, a lesson that perhaps the spirit of E.P. McGovern has learned.

NOTES

Introduction: Colorado's Supernatural Folklore

1. Von Sydow, "Geography and Folk-Tale Oicotypes," 145.
2. Von Sydow, "Geography and Folk-Tale Oicotypes."
3. Von Sydow, "Geography and Folk-Tale Oicotypes."
4. Puglia, *North American Monsters*, 6.
5. Hufford, *Terror That Comes in the Night*, 25.

1. Cowboys and Aliens: UFOs in Colorado

6. Thomas, "Usefulness of Ghost Stories," 44–52.
7. Rojcewicz, "Between One Eye Blink and the Next," 479–514.
8. Bullard, "UFO Abduction Reports," 159–65.
9. Dégh, "UFO's and How Folklorists Should Look," 244.
10 Dégh, "UFO's and How Folklorists Should Look," 244.
11. Hufford, "Beings Without Bodies," 29.
12. Hufford, *Terror That Comes in the Night*, xviii.
13. Hufford, "Beings Without Bodies," 37.
14. Dewan, "'Saucerful of Secrets'," 184.
15. Stothers, "Unidentified Flying Objects," 82.
16. "Colorado UFO Reports: UFO Report #: 1504," UFOIndex, https://www.ufoindex.com/colorado [hereafter UFOIndex].

17. Stothers, "Unidentified Flying Objects," 85.
18. "Moffatt, Colorado, September 1948—Incident Number: [ILLEGIBLE]," National Archives, https://catalog.archives.gov [hereafter National Archives].
19. "Kit Carson, Colo., September 1950," National Archives.
20. "Denver, Colorado, September 1952," National Archives.
21. Stothers, "Unidentified Flying Objects," 79.
22. Bader, "UFO Contact Movement," 74–75.
23. "Roswell UFO," FBI Records, https://vault.fbi.gov.
24. "Project BLUE BOOK—Unidentified Flying Objects," National Archives.
25. "Tioga, Colorado, June 1949—Incident Number: 370," National Archives.
26. "Manitou Springs, Colorado, August 1949," National Archives.
27. "The Condon Report: CU Boulder's Historic UFO Study," Coloradan Alumni Magazine, https://www.colorado.edu/coloradan/.
28. Cooper et al., "Glowing Auras and 'Black Money.'"
29. Chasan, "Story Behind the 'Tic Tac' UFO."
30. "Colorado UFO Reports: UFO Report #: 1002," UFOIndex.
31. Young, "When Did Fairies Get Wings?," 253.
32. Vallée, *Passport to Magonia*, 38.
33. Rojcewicz, "Between One Eye Blink and the Next," 482.
34. Dennett, *UFOs Over Colorado*, 186.
35. Dennett, *UFOs Over Colorado*, 115.
36. Rojcewicz, "Between One Eye Blink and the Next," 485.
37. Evans-Wentz, *Fairy-Faith in Celtic Countries*, 60.
38. Dennett, *UFOs Over Colorado*, 87.
39. Bullard, "UFO Abduction Reports," 156.
40. Dennett, *UFOs Over Colorado*, 103.
41. Rojcewicz, "Between One Eye Blink and the Next," 484.
42. "Colorado Springs, Colo., April 1952," National Archives, https://catalog.archives.gov/id/28941587.
43. "Colorado UFO Reports: UFO Report #: 567," UFOIndex.
44. Rojcewicz, "Between One Eye Blink and the Next," 489.
45. Dennett, *UFOs Over Colorado*, 132.
46. Rojcewicz, "Between One Eye Blink and the Next," 490.
47. Ellis, review of "UFOs in the 1980s," 254.
48. Evans-Wentz, *Fairy-Faith in Celtic Countries*, 148.
49. Shuker, *Unexplained*, 27.
50. Rojcewicz, "Between One Eye Blink and the Next," 485.

51. "Multiple Phenomena on Rocky Mountain Ranch," Above Top Secret, https://www.abovetopsecret.com.
52. Dennett, *UFOs Over Colorado*, 90.
53. Vallée, *Passport to Magonia*, 68.
54. Root, "UFOs and a Horse."
55. Vallée, *Passport to Magonia*, 52.
56. Evans-Wentz, *Fairy-Faith in Celtic Countries*, 95.
57. Rojcewicz, "'Men in Black' Experience and Tradition," 149–50.
58. Keel, *Mothman Prophecies*, 86.
59. Rojcewicz, "'Men in Black' Experience and Tradition," 148.
60. Rojcewicz, "'Men in Black' Experience and Tradition," 153–54.
61. Dennett, *UFOs Over Colorado*, 90.
62. Hufford, *Terror That Comes in the Night*, 25.
63. Hufford, "Beings Without Bodies," 37.
64. Bullard, "UFO Abduction Reports," 153.
65. Vallée, *Passport to Magonia*, 159.
66. Evans-Wentz, *Fairy-Faith in Celtic Countries*, 37.
67. Dennett, *UFOs Over Colorado*, 144.
68. Dennett, *UFOs Over Colorado*, 142.
69. Bullard, "UFO Abduction Reports," 156.
70. Dennett, *UFOs Over Colorado*, 97–98.
71. "UFOs Make Yuma Man's Life a Pit Stop," *The Denver Post*, May 8, 2007, https://www.denverpost.com.
72. Goldstein, Grider and Thomas, *Haunting Experiences*, 70.

2. "We're Going to Die Tonight": Bigfoot in Colorado

73. Out There Colorado (@outtherecolorado), "Riders on the Durango and Silverton Narrow Gauge Railroad may have spotted Bigfoot on a mountainside in Remote Colorado over the weekend. Thoughts? Video Credit: @bt92travels #bigfoot #paranormal #colorado," Instagram video.
74. Milligan, "'Truth' About the Bigfoot Legend," 85.
75. Milligan, "'Truth' About the Bigfoot Legend," 85.
76. Hufford, *Terror That Comes in the Night*, 15.
77. Hufford, "Humanoids and Anomalous Lights," 234–41.
78. Hufford, "Humanoids and Anomalous Lights," 234.
79. Hufford, "Humanoids and Anomalous Lights," 239.

80. Buhs, *Bigfoot*, 2.
81. Musharbash and Presterudstuen, *Monster Anthropology*, 5.
82. Bynum, "BIGFOOT," 352.
83. Hufford, "Humanoids and Anomalous Lights," 238.
84. Hufford, "Humanoids and Anomalous Lights," 236.
85. Loxton and Prothero, *Abominable Science!*, 40–44.
86. Hufford, "Humanoids and Anomalous Lights," 238.
87. Hufford, "Humanoids and Anomalous Lights," 240.
88. "A Monster," *Rocky Mountain News (Weekly)*, November 3, 1880.
89. "HALF MAN AND HALF BEAST," *Gunnison Democrat*, November 17, 1880.
90. Bennett, *Alas, Poor Ghost*, 36.
91. "BFRO Database History and Report Classification System," BFRO, accessed July 19, 2024, http://bfro.net/ [hereafter BFRO].
92. "Daylight Sighting by Woodsman of Two Bipeds Stalking an Elk," BFRO.
93. Oring, "Legendry and the Rhetoric," 127–66.
94. "Hunters Have an Encounter Returning from Hunt," BFRO.
95. Paddison, "Mystery of Everything Out There," 78–91.
96. Buhs, *Bigfoot*, 2009.
97. Hufford, "Humanoids and Anomalous Lights," 241.

3. Here Be Dragons: Colorado's Lake Monsters

98. "Herodotus, bk 6, logos 18," Livius, last modified on April 16, 2020, https://www.livius.org.
99. Radford and Nickell, *Lake Monster Mysteries*, 2–4.
100. Tucker, "Lake Lieberman Monster," 154–70.
101. "'Essie' Baffles Scientists; Lake Probe Planned," *The Estes Park Trail*, April 1, 1983.
102. Gabbert, "Monsters, Legends, and Festivals," 300.
103. Gabbert, "Monsters, Legends, and Festivals," 304.
104. Dickey, "Toward a Unifying Theory."
105. Dickey, "Toward a Unifying Theory."
106. "A Hideous Visitor," *Carbonate Chronicle*, June 28, 1884.
107. "The Sea Serpent Again," *The Leadville Daily/Evening Chronicle*, August 3, 1894.
108. "Hideous Visitor."
109. "Down in the Depths," *Carbonate Chronicle*, July 12, 1884.
110. "Down in the Depths."

111. "What the Cottonwood Sea Serpent Really Is," *Colorado Republican*, August 22, 1907.
112. "What the Cottonwood Sea Serpent Really Is."
113. "What the Cottonwood Sea Serpent Really Is."
114. "What the Cottonwood Sea Serpent Really Is."
115. "What the Cottonwood Sea Serpent Really Is."
116. "What the Cottonwood Sea Serpent Really Is."
117. "Westminster Enquirer," Facebook, July 20, 2016, https://www.facebook.com.
118. Garcia, "Desire to Find 'Standley Lake Monster.'"
119. Garcia, "Desire to Find 'Standley Lake Monster.'"
120. "'Monster' Reported at Lake Katherine," *Aspen Times (weekly)*, October 25, 1979.
121. "Grand Lake Sea-Serpent," *Georgetown Courier*, September 17, 1885.
122. "The Legend of Grand Lake," Grand Lake Area Historical Society, accessed July 18, 2024, https://grandlakehistory.org
123. "Legend of Grand Lake."
124. "Lakes Monitoring," Colorado Department of Public Health and Environment, accessed July 18, 2024, https://cdphe.colorado.gov.

4. Knock, Knock, Who's There? Colorado's Tommyknockers

125. James, "Knockers, Knackers, and Ghosts," 154.
126. James, "Knockers, Knackers, and Ghosts," 157.
127. Bottrell, *Traditions and Hearthside Stories*, 186–89.
128. Kingsley, *Yeast*, 1888.
129. James, *Folklore of Cornwall*, 157.
130. Hunt, *Popular Romances*, 88.
131. James, "Knockers, Knackers, and Ghosts," 158.
132. Hunt, *Popular Romances*, 346–49.
133. James, *Folklore of Cornwall*, 157.
134. Puglia, *North American Monsters*, 16.
135. Puglia, *North American Monsters*, 8.
136. James, *Folklore of Cornwall*, 150.
137. Von Sydow, *Selected Papers on Folklore*, 11.
138. James, *Folklore of Cornwall*, 159.
139. Hand, "California Miners' Folklore," 128–29.

140. Hand, "Folklore from Utah's Silver Mining," 143.
141. Bancroft, "Folklore of the Central City District," 316.
142. Bancroft, "Folklore of the Central City District," 315.
143. Bancroft, "Folklore of the Central City District," 320.
144. Bancroft, "Folklore of the Central City District," 322.
145. Hand, "Folklore from Utah's Silver Mining," 142.
146. Bancroft, "Folklore of the Central City District," 328.
147. James, *Folklore of Cornwall*, 159.
148. Vitaliano, "Geomythology," 5.
149. Puglia, *North American Monsters*, 7.
150. James, *Folklore of Cornwall*, 157.
151. Bancroft, "Folklore of the Central City District," 332.
152. Tolbert and Brodie, "Ostension."
153. Dégh and Vázsonyi, "Does the Word 'Dog' Bite?," 5–34.
154. Tolbert and Brodie, "Ostension."
155. Bancroft, "Folklore of the Central City District," 333.
156. Bancroft, "Folklore of the Central City District," 322.
157. Patton and Matthews, "Marketing American Microbrews," 24.
158. Shortridge, "Keeping Tabs on Kansas," 10.
159. Cohen, "Monster Culture," 199.
160. Ellis, "Legend Tripping in Ohio," 69.
161. Koven, *Film, Folklore, and Urban Legends*, 159.
162. Ellis, "Legend Tripping in Ohio," 489.
163. Thigpen, "Adolescent Legends in Brown County," 204–5.
164. Adams, "Folk Narrative," 23.
165. Ellis, "Legend Tripping in Ohio," 66–67.
166. Goldstein, Grider and Thomas, *Haunting Experiences*, 186–89.
167. *Ghost Adventures*, season 13, episode 1, "Colorado Gold Mine," aired September 24, 2016, on Travel Channel [hereafter *Ghost Adventures*, "Colorado Gold Mine"].
168. *Ghost Adventures*, "Colorado Gold Mine."
169. Koven, *Film, Folklore, and Urban Legends*, 156.
170. *Ghost Adventures*, "Colorado Gold Mine."
171. *Ghost Adventures*, "Colorado Gold Mine."
172. *Ghost Adventures*, "Colorado Gold Mine."
173. *Ghost Adventures*, "Colorado Gold Mine."
174. *Ghost Adventures*, "Colorado Gold Mine."
175. *Ghost Adventures*, "Colorado Gold Mine."
176. Thomas, "Usefulness of Ghost Stories," 44–52.

5. Fantastic Beasts of Colorado and Where to Find Them: A Colorado Bestiary

177. Dendle, "Cryptozoology in the Medieval," 1.
178. Cohen, "Monster Culture," 199.
179. Hurn, *Anthropology and Cryptozoology*, 1.
180. Heuvelmans, "How Many Animal Species Remain," 5.
181. Ives, "Folklore of Eastern Middle Park," 29–30.
182. Ives, "Folklore of Eastern Middle Park," 30.
183. Ives, "Folklore of Eastern Middle Park," 30.
184. Rettig, "Tracing the Source of Irrigation," 2.
185. Ives, "Folklore of Eastern Middle Park," 30.
186. "NADP Encounters Map," North American Dogman Project, accessed December 13, 2024, https://northamericandogmanproject.com [herafter NADP].
187. NADP Encounters Map," NADP.
188. Getz, *Weird Colorado*, 110–11.
189. Getz, *Weird Colorado*, 110.
190. Ellis, *Aliens*, 13.
191. Dégh, *Legend and Belief*, 252–53.
192. Brunvand, *Vanishing Hitchhiker*, 50–51.
193. Brunvand, *Vanishing Hitchhiker*, 200–01.
194. Cox, *Fearsome Creatures of the Lumberwoods*, 21.
195. "The Slide-Rock Bolter," Wandering the Whale Road, October 12, 2017, https://wanderingwhaleroad.wordpress.com.
196. "Slide-Rock Bolter."
197. "#119 Rita the Rock Planter," Thomas Dambo, accessed December 16, 2024, https://www.thomasdambo.com
198. Lindow, *Trolls*, 51.
199. Lindow, *Trolls*, 54.
200. "There's a Vampire Buried in Lafayette?," 9News, January 16, 2015, https://www.9news.com.
201. "Vampire Grave of Lafayette," Atlas Obscura, accessed December 16, 2024, https://www.atlasobscura.com.
202. "The Lafayette Vampire," Rocky Mountain Paranormal, accessed December 16, 2024, https://www.rockymountainparanormal.com.
203. Barber, *Vampires*, 2.
204. Barber, *Vampires*, 2.
205. Barber, *Vampires*, 2.

206. Barber, *Vampires*, 6–7.
207. Barber, *Vampires*, 6–7.
208. "Legends of the Dunes: Webfooted Horses and Singing Sand," The Pueblo Chieftain, accessed December 16, 2024, https://www.chieftain.com.

6. The Colorado Horror: Haunted Houses

209. Briggs, *Dictionary of Fairies*, 13.
210. Glassie, "Folkloristic Study of the American Artifact," 378.
211. Bailey, *American Nightmares*, 114.
212. Goldstein, Grider and Thomas, *Haunting Experiences*, 149.
213. Bailey, *American Nightmares*, 3.
214. Goldstein, Grider and Thomas, *Haunting Experiences*, 146.
215. Bailey, *American Nightmares*, 114.
216. Edwards, "Ten Spooky Stories."
217. Goldstein, Grider and Thomas, *Haunting Experiences*, 152–56.
218. Iversen, *Molly Brown*, xvi.
219. Fisher, "What Is Hauntology?," 19.
220. Rhodes, "Haunted Happenings."
221. Rhodes, "Haunted Happenings."
222. Thompson, *Motif-Index*, 934.
223. Bailey, *American Nightmares*, 114.
224. "Haunted Homes of Capitol Hill," *Denver Like a Local Tours*.
225. Melrose, "Haunted House."
226. Melrose, "Haunted House."
227. Melrose, "Haunted House."
228. Melrose, "Haunted House."
229. "Notorious 'Haunted House' Is Leased by Denver for Isolation Hospital," *Rocky Mountain News*, August 15, 1923.
230. Bailey, *American Nightmares*, 56.
231. Bailey, *American Nightmares*, 56.
232. Rudolph, "Haunting at Bradmar."
233. Bradley and Bradley, *Psychic Phenomena*, 26.
234. Rudolph, "Haunting at Bradmar."
235. Bradley and Bradley, *Psychic Phenomena*, 8.
236. Rudolph, "Denver House That Inspired."
237. Goldstein, Grider and Thomas, *Haunting Experiences*, 30–44.
238. Goldstein, Grider and Thomas, *Haunting Experiences*, 36.

239. Goldstein, Grider and Thomas, *Haunting Experiences*, 36.
240. Goldstein, Grider and Thomas, *Haunting Experiences*, 37.
241. Goldstein, Grider and Thomas, *Haunting Experiences*, 37.

7. On the Road Again: Riverdale Road

242. McNeill and Tucker, *Legend Tripping*, 11–12.
243. Ellis, "Legend Tripping in Ohio," 64.
244. McNeill and Tucker, *Legend Tripping*, 16–19.
245. White, *Haunted Roads*, 16.
246. Sylte, "One of the Most Haunted Roads."
247. McNeill and Tucker, *Legend Tripping*, 6.
248. White, *Haunted Roads*, 11.
249. "The Gates of Hell," Colorado Urban Legends, September 12, 2016, http://www.coloradourbanlegends.com/.
250. Rudolph, "David Wolpert House."
251. Rudolph, "David Wolpert House."
252. Thompson, *Motif-Index*.
253. Seemann, "'Char-Man'," 91.
254. Haring and Breslerman, "Cropsey Maniac," 61.
255. "What Haunts Riverdale Road?" Factschology, https://factschology.com.
256. Bennett and Smith, *Contemporary Legend*, 287.
257. Goldstein, Grider and Thomas, *Haunting Experiences*, 54–55.
258. Bradley, "8 Facts About Riverdale Road."
259. Bennett and Smith, *Contemporary Legend*, 292.
260. Bradley, "8 Facts About Riverdale Road."
261. Bennett and Smith, *Contemporary Legend*, 209–10.
262. Sylte, "One of the Most Haunted Roads."
263. White, *Haunted Roads*, 15.

8. Specters of Parks: Haunted Places

264. Goldstein, Grider and Thomas, *Haunting Experiences*, 183.
265. Goldstein, Grider and Thomas, *Haunting Experiences*, 174.
266. "Haunted Hotel History," The Stanley Hotel, accessed December 16, 2024, https://web.archive.org/web/20150602065100/http://www.stanleyhotel.com/hauntedhistory.

267. @amodernnomad, "Intelligent spirit Lucy pushes lollipop up at the Stanley Hotel!," TikTok, August 12, 2021, https://www.tiktok.com.
268. "Stanley Ghost Stories Shine with Authenticity," The Stanley Hotel, accessed December 16, 2024, https://web.archive.org/web/20130712052953/http://www.stanleyhotel.com/media-center/Stanley-Ghost-Stories-Shine-with-Authenticity.
269. Fisher, "What Is Hauntology?," 19.
270. Fisher, "What Is Hauntology?," 20.
271. Goldstein, Grider and Thomas, *Haunting Experiences*.
272. Tolbert and Foster, *Möbius Media*.
273. Ashliman, "Devil's Bridge."
274. Dégh, "Haunted Bridges Near Avon and Danville," 77–81.
275. McNeill and Tucker, *Legend Tripping*, 34.
276. Jones, *Sand Creek Massacre*, 11.
277. Jones, *Sand Creek Massacre*, 23.
278. Jones, *Sand Creek Massacre*, 23.
279. Kovaleski, "Other Teens Crashed."
280. Baughman, *Type and Motif-Index*, 147.
281. Kovaleski, "Other Teens Crashed."
282. McNeill and Tucker, *Legend Tripping*, 34.
283. "Third Bridge (Colorado)," Reddit, 2016, https://www.reddit.com/r/Paranormal.
284. McNeill and Tucker, *Legend Tripping*, 63.
285. "Third Bridge—Real Bennett Haunt," Co Haunted Houses, accessed December 16, 2024, https://www.cohauntedhouses.com.
286. "Third Bridge—Real."
287. "The Work of Ghouls," *Denver Republican*, March 19, 1893.
288. "Cheesman," City and County of Denver, accessed December 16, 2024, https://web.archive.org/web/20081017214528/http://www.denvergov.org/CheesmanPark/tabid/380771/Default.aspx.

BIBLIOGRAPHY

Adams, Linda Kinsey. "Folk Narrative." In *The Emergence of Folklore in Everyday Life: A Field Guide and Sourcebook*, edited by George H. Shoemaker. Trickster Press, 1990.

Alexander, J.H. *The Legend of the Blue-Dillon Monster: An Apocryphal Tale*. Blue-Dillon Research Society, LLC, 2010.

Ashliman, D.L. "The Devil's Bridge." Accessed December 16, 2024. https://sites.pitt.edu/~dash/type1191.html.

Bader, Chris D. "The UFO Contact Movement from the 1950s to the Present." *Studies in Popular Culture* 17, no. 2 (1995): 73–90.

Bailey, Dale. *American Nightmares: The Haunted House Formula in American Popular Fiction*. University of Wisconsin Press, 2011.

Bancroft, Caroline. "Folklore of the Central City District, Colorado." *California Folklore Quarterly* 4, no. 4 (1945): 315–42.

Barber, Paul. *Vampires, Burial, and Death: Folklore and Reality*. Yale University Press, 1988.

Baughman, Ernest W. *Type and Motif-Index of the Folktales of England and North America*. De Gruyter, 1966.

Bennett, Gillian. *Alas, Poor Ghost*. University Press of Colorado, 1999.

Bennett, Gillian, and Paul Smith. *Contemporary Legend: A Reader*. Routledge, 2013.

Bottrell, William. *Traditions and Hearthside Stories of West Cornwall*. Beare and Son, 1873.

Bradley, Dorothy Bomar, and Robert A. Bradley. *Psychic Phenomena: Revelations and Experiences*. Paperback Library, 1967.

Bradley, Kacey. "8 Facts about Riverdale Road, The Most Terrifying Place in Colorado You've Never Been To." Thought Catalog, June 24, 2021, https://thoughtcatalog.com.

Briggs, Katharine Mary. *A Dictionary of Fairies: Hobgoblins, Brownies, Bogies, and Other Supernatural Creatures*. Pantheon Books, 1976.

Brunvand, Jan Harold. *The Vanishing Hitchhiker: American Urban Legends and Their Meanings*. W.W. Norton & Company, 1981.

Buhs, Joshua Blu. *Bigfoot: The Life and Times of a Legend*. University of Chicago Press, 2009.

Bullard, Thomas. "UFO Abduction Reports: The Supernatural Kidnap Narrative Returns in Technological Guise." *Journal of American Folklore* 102, no. 404 (June 1989): 159–65.

Bynum, Joyce. "BIGFOOT—A Contemporary Belief Legend." *ETC: A Review of General Semantics* 49, no. 3 (1992): 352–57.

Chasan, Aliza. "The Story Behind the 'Tic Tac' UFO Sighting by Navy Pilots in 2004." CBS News. https://www.cbsnews.com.

Cohen, Jeffrey Jerome. "Monster Culture (Seven Theses)." *Gothic Horror: A Guide for Students and Readers* (2007): 198–216.

Cooper, Helene, et al. "Glowing Auras and 'Black Money': The Pentagon's Mysterious U.F.O. Program." *New York Times*, December 16, 2017. https://www.nytimes.com.

Cox, William T. *Fearsome Creatures of the Lumberwoods: With a Few Desert and Mountain Beasts*. Press of Judd & Detweiler, Incorporated, 1910.

Dégh, Linda. "The Haunted Bridges Near Avon and Danville and Their Role in Legend Formation." *Indiana Folklore* 2 (1): 77–81.

———. *Legend and Belief: Dialectics of a Folklore Genre*. Indiana University Press, 2001.

———. "UFO's and How Folklorists Should Look at Them." *Fabula* (1977): 242–48.

Dégh, Linda, and Andrew Vázsonyi. "Does the Word 'Dog' Bite? Ostensive Action: A Means of Legend-Telling." *Journal of Folklore Research* 20, no. 1 (1983): 5-34.

Dendle, Peter. "Cryptozoology in the Medieval and Modern Worlds." *Folklore* 117, no. 2 (2006): 190–206.

Dennett, Preston. *UFOs Over Colorado: A True History of Extraterrestrial Encounters in the Centennial State*. Schiffer Publishing, 2017.

Dewan, William J. "'A Saucerful of Secrets': An Interdisciplinary Analysis of UFO Experiences." *Journal of American Folklore* 119, no. 472 (2006): 184–202.

Dickey, Colin. "Toward a Unifying Theory of Lake Monsters." Atlas Obscura, January 17, 2024. https://www.atlasobscura.com.

Dorson, Richard. *Man and Beast in American Comic Legend*. Indiana University Press, 1982.

Dundes, Alan. *International Folkloristics: Classic Contributions by the Founders of Folklore*. Rowman and Littlefield Publishers, 1999.

Edwards, Robin. "Ten Spooky Stories from Denver's Croke-Patterson Mansion." *Westword*, October 27, 2011.

Ellis, Bill. *Aliens, Ghosts, and Cults*. University Press of Mississippi, 2003.

———. "Legend Tripping in Ohio." In *Legend Tripping: A Contemporary Legend Casebook*, edited by Lynne S. McNeill and Elizabeth Tucker. University Press of Colorado, 2018.

———. Review of "UFOs in the 1980s: The UFO Encyclopedia," by Jerome Clark. *Journal of American Folklore* 105, no. 416 (Spring 1992): 252–55

Evans-Wentz, W.Y. *The Fairy-Faith in Celtic Countries*. Oxford University Press, 1911.

Fisher, Mark. "What Is Hauntology?" *Film Quarterly* 66, no. 1 (2012): 16–24.

Gabbert, Lisa. "Monsters, Legends, and Festivals." In *North American Monsters: A Contemporary Legend Casebook*, edited by David Puglia. University Press of Colorado, 2022.

Garcia, Peyton. "Desire to find 'Standley Lake Monster' Draws Residents to Westminster Trails and Open Spaces." *Denver Post*, October 31, 2017. https://www.denverpost.com.

Getz, Charmaine Ortega. *Weird Colorado.* Sterling Publishing, 2010.

Glassie, Henry. "Folkloristic Study of the American Artifact: Objects and Objectives." In *Handbook of American Folklore*, edited by Richard Dorson. Indiana University Press, 1983.

Goldstein, Diane, Sylvia Grider, and Jeannie Banks Thomas. *Haunting Experiences: Ghosts in Contemporary Folklore*. University Press of Colorado, 2007.

Hand, Wayland D. "California Miners' Folklore: Below Ground." *California Folklore Quarterly* 1, no. 2 (1942): 127–53.

———. "Folklore from Utah's Silver Mining Camps." *Journal of American Folklore* 54, nos. 213/214 (1941): 132–61.

Haring, Lee, and Mark Breslerman. "The Cropsey Maniac." In *North American Monsters: A Contemporary Legend Casebook*, edited by David Puglia. University Press of Colorado, 2022.

Heuvelmans, Bernard. "How Many Animal Species Remain to Be Discovered." *Cryptozoology* 2 (1983): 5.

Hufford, David. "Beings Without Bodies: An Experience-Centered Theory of the Belief in Spirits." In *Out of the Ordinary: Folklore and the Supernatural*, edited by Barbara Walker. University Press of Colorado, 1995.

———. "Humanoids and Anomalous Lights: Taxonomic and Epistemological Problems." *Fabula* 18, no. 3 (1977): 234–41.

———. *The Terror That Comes in the Night: An Experience-Centered Study of Supernatural Assault Traditions*. University of Pennsylvania Press, 1982.

Hunt, Robert. *Popular Romances of the West of England, or, The Drolls, Traditions, and Superstitions of Old Cornwall*. Chatto & Windus, 1908.

Hurn, Samantha. *Anthropology and Cryptozoology: Exploring Encounters with Mysterious Creatures*. Taylor & Francis, 2016.

Iversen, Kristen. *Molly Brown: Unraveling the Myth*. Big Earth Publishing, 1999.

Ives, Ronald L. "Folklore of Eastern Middle Park, Colorado." *Journal of American Folklore* 54, nos. 211/212 (1941): 24–43.

James, Ronald M. *The Folklore of Cornwall: The Oral Tradition of a Celtic Nation*. University of Exeter Press, 2019.

———. "Knockers, Knackers, and Ghosts: Immigrant Folklore in the Western Mines." *Western Folklore* 51, no. 2 (1992): 153–77.

Jones, Larry W. *Sand Creek Massacre*. Lulu, 2023.

Keel, John. *The Mothman Prophecies*. Tor Books, 1975.

Kingsley, Charles. *Yeast: A Problem*. Macmillan, 1888.

Kovaleski, Jennifer Lee. "Other Teens Crashed at 'Third Bridge' Years Before Deadly Accident That Killed Five." Denver 7, October 4, 2016. https://www.denver7.com.

Koven, Mikel J. *Film, Folklore, and Urban Legends*. Scarecrow Press, 2008.

Lawless, Elaine J. *Holy Women, Wholly Women: Sharing Ministries of Wholeness Through Life Stories and Reciprocal Ethnography*. University of Pennsylvania Press, 1993.

Lindow, John. *Trolls: An Unnatural History*. Reaktion Books, 2014.

Loxton, Daniel, and Donald R. Prothero. *Abominable Science! Origins of the Yeti, Nessie, and Other Famous Cryptids*. Columbia University Press, 2013.

MacDougall, Curtis Daniel. *Hoaxes*. Dover Publications, 1958.

McNeill, Lynne S., and Elizabeth Tucker, eds. *Legend Tripping: A Contemporary Legend Casebook*. University Press of Colorado, 2018.

Melrose, Frances. "The Haunted House." *Rocky Mountain News*, March 14, 1948.

Milligan, Linda. "'The Truth' About the Bigfoot Legend." *Western Folklore* 49, no. 1 (1990): 83–98.

Musharbash, Yasmine, and G. Presterudstuen, eds. *Monster Anthropology in Australasia and Beyond*. Springer, 2014.

Oring, Elliott. "Legendry and the Rhetoric of Truth." *Journal of American Folklore* 121, no. 480 (2008): 127–66.

Paddison, Joshua. "The Mystery of Everything Out There: Bigfoot and Religion in the 21st Century." In *The Paranormal and Popular Culture*. Routledge, 2019.

Patton, Matthew T., and Adam J. Matthews. "Marketing American Microbrews: Promoting Neolocalism One Map At a Time." In *Papers in Applied Geography* 36 (2013).

Puglia, David. *North American Monsters: A Contemporary Legend Casebook*. University of Colorado Press, 2022.

Radford, Benjamin, and Joe Nickell. *Lake Monster Mysteries: Investigating the World's Most Elusive Creatures*. University Press of Kentucky, 2006.

Renoux, Matt. "'A Heck of a Sea Monster': The Story Behind the Creature Spotted on Dillon Reservoir." 9News, April 21, 2020, https://www.9news.com.

Rettig, Patricia J. "Tracing the Source of Irrigation: An Examination of Colorado Ditch Company Collections in Archival Repositories." *Journal of Western Archives* 3, no. 1 (2012): 1–20.

Rhodes, Maddie. "Haunted Happenings at the Molly Brown House, as Told by the Museum Director." *Fox31 Denver*, October 2023.

Rojcewicz, Peter M. "Between One Eye Blink and the Next: Fairies, UFOs, and Problems of Knowledge." In *The Good People: New Fairylore Essays*, edited by Peter Narvaez. University Press of Kentucky, 1991.

———. "The 'Men in Black' Experience and Tradition: Analogues With the Traditional Devil Hypothesis." *Journal of American Folklore* (1987): 148–60.

Root, Chris. "UFOs and a Horse Called Snippy." Denver Public Library Special Collections and Archives. https://history.denverlibrary.org.

Rudolph, Katie. "The David Wolpert House: Dissecting A Riverdale Road Ghost Story." Denver Public Library Special Collections and Archives, October 29, 2019. https://history.denverlibrary.org.

———. "A Denver House That Inspired a Horror Film." Denver Public Library Special Collections and Archives, October 22, 2013. https://history.denverlibrary.org.

———. "The Haunting at Bradmar." Denver Public Library Special Collections and Archives, October 31, 2018. https://history.denverlibrary.org.

———. "Newspaper Reports of a Haunted House, 1902–1904." Denver Public Library Special Collections and Archives, October 17, 2014. https://history.denverlibrary.org.

Schwartz, Alvin. *Kickle Snifters and Other Fearsome Critters*. HarperCollins Publishers, 1976.

Seemann, Charlie. "The 'Char-Man'." In *North American Monsters: A Contemporary Legend Casebook*, edited by David Puglia. University Press of Colorado, 2022.

Shortridge, James R. "Keeping Tabs on Kansas: Reflections on Regionally Based Field Study." *Journal of Cultural Geography* 16, no. 1 (1996): 5–16.

Shuker, Karl P.N. *The Unexplained: An Illustrated Guide to the World's Paranormal Mysteries*. Metro Books, 2009.

Stothers, Richard. "Unidentified Flying Objects in Classical Antiquity." *Classical Journal* 103, no. 1 (2007): 79–92.

Sylte, Allison. "One of the Most Haunted Roads in the US Is Just a Few Miles from Denver." 9News, October 10, 2022. https://www.9news.com.

Thigpen, Kenneth A., Jr. "Adolescent Legends in Brown County: A Survey." *Indiana Folklore* 4, no. 2 (1971): 141–215.

Thomas, Jeannie Banks. "The Usefulness of Ghost Stories." In *Haunting Experiences: Ghosts in Contemporary Folklore*. Utah State University Press, 2007.

Thompson, Stith. *Motif-Index of Folk-Literature*. Indiana University Press, 1960.

Tolbert, Jeffrey A., and Ian Brodie. "Ostension." In *Sage Research Methods Foundations*, edited by Paul Atkinson, Sara Delamont, Alexandru Cernat, Joseph W. Sakshaug and Richard A. Williams. SAGE Publications Ltd., 2019.

Tolbert, Jeffrey A., and Michael Dylan Foster, eds. *Möbius Media: Popular Culture, Folklore, and the Folkloresque*. University Press of Colorado, 2024.

Tucker, Elizabeth. "The Lake Lieberman Monster." In *North American Monsters: A Contemporary Legend Casebook*, edited by David Puglia. University Press of Colorado, 2022.

Vallée, Jacques. *Passport to Magonia: From Folklore to Flying Saucers*. Daily Grail Publishing, 1969.

Vitaliano, Dorothy B. "Geomythology: The Impact of Geologic Events on History and Legend with Special Reference to Atlantis." *Journal of the Folklore Institute* 5, no. 1 (1968): 5–30.

Von Sydow, Carl Wilhelm. "Geography and Folk-Tale Oicotypes." In *International Folkloristics: Classic Contributions by the Founders of Folklore*, edited by Alan Dundes. Rowman and Littlefield Publishers, 1999.

———. *Selected Papers on Folklore*. Rosenkilde and Bagger, 1948.

White, Thomas. *Haunted Roads of Western Pennsylvania*. The History Press, 2015.
Young, Simon. "When Did Fairies Get Wings?" In *The Paranormal and Popular Culture*, edited by Daryl Caterine and John W. Morehead. Routledge, 2019.

ABOUT THE AUTHOR

Jack Daly is a folklorist from Evergreen who currently resides in Westminster, Colorado. Jack is a PhD candidate in American Studies at Pennsylvania State University at Harrisburg, where he was the recipient of the prestigious University Graduate Fellowship. He has a master's degree in folklore from Utah State University, as well as bachelor's degrees in English, history and anthropology from the University of Kansas. In 2023, he was the recipient of the Warren E. Roberts prize for best paper on Folk Art and Material Culture from the American Folklore Society. His work has been published in *The Journal of American Folklore*, *The Journal of Folklore Research*, *Western Folklore* and *The Journal of Scientific Exploration*, and has forthcoming publications in *Contemporary Legend* and *The Folklore Historian*. He has taught at Pennsylvania State University, Utah State University, the University of Colorado at Boulder and Front Range Community College. While not researching monsters and the supernatural, Jack enjoys spending time with his wife, Carly, and cat Little Missy, birdwatching at Stanley Lake, hiking in the mountains and cheering on the Broncos.